Institutional Theory and Organizational Change

Institutional Theory and Organizational Change

Staffan Furusten

Associate Professor in Management, Stockholm School of Economics and Director, Stockholm Centre for Organizational Research (Score), Sweden

Edward Elgar

Cheltenham, UK • Northampton, MA, USA

© Staffan Furusten 2013

First published in Swedish as *Den Institutionella Omvärlden*, Lund: Liber
© Staffan Furusten 2007
Translated by Kelly Vegh Olsson

Published by
Edward Elgar Publishing Limited
The Lypiatts
15 Lansdown Road
Cheltenham
Glos GL50 2JA
UK

Edward Elgar Publishing, Inc.
William Pratt House
9 Dewey Court
Northampton
Massachusetts 01060
USA

A catalogue record for this book
is available from the British Library

Library of Congress Control Number: 2013932989

This book is available electronically in the ElgarOnline.com Business
Subject Collection, E-ISBN 978 1 78254 709 9

ISBN 978 1 78254 708 2 (cased)

Typeset by Columns Design XML Ltd, Reading
Printed and bound in Great Britain by T.J. International Ltd, Padstow

Contents

Preface

Since the early 1980s, institutional organization theory has become increasingly established as a way of explaining how organizations work in interaction with the world around them. Many studies have been conducted and numerous scientific publications have been produced. For over a decade, institutional organization theory has been used – for example, at the Stockholm School of Economics, the academic environment I am most familiar with – as a central theory starting in first-term courses where the relationships between businesses and their environment are studied. However, both teachers and students have experienced a shortage of literature that takes a more general approach to the studies conducted over the years. Attempts to summarize the current state of research and package it into a single format have been few. And even if these attempts are commendable and work well at the graduate and doctoral level, they have not been very accessible to a wider audience.

This book is based on lectures I have given for a number of years at Stockholm School of Economics, in a course on organizational change. Over the years, the idea to compile the main theme developed in these lectures into a book slowly took shape, and a first version in Swedish was published by Liber in 2007. It is important to note that the book does not claim to be an exhaustive review of institutional organization theory or to present everything that has been done in the field from the late 1970s onward. The ambition is, rather, to describe what the institutional environment is made up of and how organizations are governed by it.

Although it is my hand on the pen (or rather, the keyboard), the book must be seen as a product of the research environment in which it was written: Score (Stockholm Centre for Organizational Research), a joint multi–disciplinary research centre of Stockholm School of Economics and Stockholm University. The course from which the idea of the book arose was originally developed by me in cooperation with Karin Fernler, Bengt Jacobsson and Nils Brunsson. These people have therefore been a key source of inspiration, though all of my colleagues at Score have contributed directly or indirectly to my writing of this book. Many conversations with John Meyer over the years also inspired me to finally sit down and write a book on institutional theory and organizational change.

1. Organizing beyond management and market

Similar façades but different foundations

Anyone who travels the world quickly discovers that there are many similarities between countries with respect to what they look like and how they work. We see, for example, a great likeness in the foods people eat. McDonald's restaurants can be found in cities worldwide, and pizzerias are everywhere from small Swedish communities like Forshaga (north of Karlstad) and Mölnbo on the outskirts of Södertälje with only a few thousand residents, to global metropolises with millions. Soft drinks like Coca-Cola and Fanta can also be purchased almost everywhere around the globe. From a local perspective, in this case Sweden, for many families Fridays are associated with a laid-back evening with Mexican food. No tacos – no cosy Friday dinners!

The similarities between what goes on in different places are found in many different areas. For example, all across the world people listen to the same kind of music, even if there may also be a local variety of music characteristic of a particular region. However, even this is subject to globalization under the label of 'ethno-music'. We also see the same clothing styles wherever we go. Local variations naturally exist, but if we look at how people dress in urban centres around the world, the similarities are striking. For example, in Sweden in the early years of the 2010s, children and seniors alike are wearing NY Yankees baseball caps!

It is interesting to note that even when we try to be different, we tend to do things in similar ways no matter where we are in the world. Global subcultures have been established, where distinctive lifestyle standards determine whether we belong to one culture or another. Even if we rebel and do our best to be unique, we do it in the same way, such as listening to the same alternative music, wearing the same alternative clothes and symbols, and in other ways embracing certain approaches to situations and things (for example, flower power, punk, heavy metal, hip hop, piercing, tattoos, Goth rock, etc.).

Similarities are seen not only in food, clothes and music, but also when it comes to other things. Architecture is one example. During different time periods, every big city claiming to be a modern urban centre shows striking similarities in the appearance of their buildings. Beijing, for example, has undergone a dramatic change in the last 20 years, with its characteristic low buildings and narrow lanes suited to bicycles being replaced by Western-style skyscrapers and wide roads for cars. Yes, even Beijing has taken on a typically American 'downtown' look! We also watch the same TV shows and movies, and read the same books, newspapers and magazines. We see the same round-the-clock news on CNN or the BBC, and use the same software programs and types of computers. Almost every large city has a metro, and airports all look the same. There are organizations that promote equal working conditions across the world (for example, the International Labour Organization, ILO), equality, health (for example, the World Health Organization, WHO), free trade (for example, the World Trade Organization, WTO), and the like. From a Swedish viewpoint, the EU is a familiar and tangible example of one such organization where common rules and conditions are drawn up for citizens and organizations, public and private, in the EU member states. When you renew your passport in Sweden today, for example, the new one states that you are a citizen of the European Union.

We also see education becoming more and more synchronized and standardized between nations so that we all compete on the same playing field in global labour markets. By way of the so-called 'Bologna model', the aim is for us to have access to the same educations, with the same content, that lead to the same degrees, regardless of where we live in Europe. Another example of similarity is that the organization of both public and private activities is becoming increasingly standardized around the world, allowing us to compare the performance of organizations. We use the same measures of organizational quality across the world. The *Financial Times*, for example, has developed a model for ranking business schools and their masters programs, executive education and MBAs around the world. To make these lists, educational institutions must therefore offer programs that are measurable; that is, that meet the criteria measured by the ranking system. Organizations also use the same ideas of organization and management around the world. Popular models such as Business Process Reengineering, Total Quality Management, Balanced Scorecard, Shareholder Value, Time-based Management, Corporate Social Responsibility, etc., are discussed and tested in many organizations in a lot of countries at the same time. Among the means used to spread organizational ideas are books, with the result that some management books that promote specific management models and leadership styles are sold in vast numbers (millions) across the entire world. In addition, US consulting firms and large companies from many countries operate their business on a global basis, also contributing to the diffusion of certain organizational and management ideas to many organizations around the world.

Despite the above emphasis on the tendencies toward international similarity, I have also hinted at the existence of elements of local variation in different cultures. But variations exist not only in how central local religions, local customs or laws are. At the same time as tendencies toward increased similarity are strong globally, there are also local variations that on the surface appear to be similar. In other words, it is not unusual for us to interpret different meanings in different contexts, for example, of a management model. That is, the same idea about education may be advocated in many countries, but the practice that it leads to can be fundamentally different. The curriculum may be copied in many countries, with a certain country seen as having come a long way using it as a starting point, but what then takes place in the classroom can vary considerably. That is, just because the US secondary school curriculum was used as a template for school reforms in Botswana does not mean that the teaching offered there is particularly like that offered at US secondary schools.[1]

Different places around the world also exhibit differences in culture and legislation, meaning that even if there are obvious similarities on the surface in some contexts, such as education, the differences in cultural conditions can be considerable. Consequently, the formation of the activities being carried out may differ with respect to the importance given, for example, to the advice of a US management consultant, a management model described in a popular book, an international standard for quality or environmental management ...

The idea of the book

The idea of this book is to show that we, as individuals and as a collective, cannot isolate ourselves from what is going on around us. We are affected by tendencies toward greater similarity in many respects across the world, but we are also affected by local cultural factors. This applies both in our private lives and in the workplace; and to companies, associations, government agencies, and individuals. We cannot avoid these influences, and this applies both to us as individuals and to those whose job it is to lead us. This means that managers are not omnipotent or able to do whatever they want in a given situation. That which falls within the realm of possibility is determined by what was described earlier as tendencies toward globalization, and local variations in culture and how global trends are received locally.

The 'institutional environment' of organizations is the concept used here to describe such circumstances, and shall thus be understood as the surrounding environment that determines the conditions that organizations and their managers must adapt to and manage in order to be regarded as legitimate actors in the type of business they conduct. If the business is education, this means that each and every school must live up to the institutional demands for what is considered to characterize a real school. If the business is steel production, the organization must live up to the institutional demands for what is considered to characterize a real steel manufacturer. In the case of hospitals, the organization must meet the institutional demands for what is considered to characterize a real hospital, etc.

These demands remain fairly constant over time. This is also what is meant by the concept of 'institutionalization' – that is, where an activity has become so established that most of us take for granted a certain understanding of what characterizes education, steel production, or hospital care, for example. If, in addition, there is legislation to support these institutionalized understandings, the likelihood is great that they will live on for a long time. Such understandings are, however, not static. They are constantly being influenced and modified by tendencies, as described above, toward a global convergence of ideas about organizing and management. Prior to the 1980s, for example, it was not a given in the West that market mechanisms should control the allocation of resources in health care and education. At the beginning of the 2000s, it is almost the opposite – that is, it is seen as strange for a state to allocate resources to hospitals and schools according to a policy-driven distribution model.

Amidst all this noise of impressions and institutions, are the decision-makers. Decision-makers are needed, but that they themselves control the nature and timing of their decisions is doubtful. This book argues that policy-makers make the decisions that are possible according to the institutional framework of their organizations, and that they do this whether they like it or not, and whether they are aware of it or not. With a better understanding of the environment around these decision-makers, and how it affects how they think, what they do and why they do it, they also improve their chances of making more carefully considered decisions.

This book is written from an organizational perspective, which means that the arguments are based on how organizations work and why things are done in a certain way in organizations. The aim is to specify key elements in the environment where individual organizations and their decision-makers operate, and to discuss the importance of these elements in the shaping and development of the activities an organization engages in. Here, we are dealing with variables and connections that can be perceived as abstract and thereby also as elusive, and therefore perhaps at first glance even unimportant or self-evident. The reason for this is that elements in the institutional environment are difficult to discern, and it is difficult to identify clear, measurable links between what goes on in the institutional environment and how individual organizations develop.

How is it then that what we can't see is important for what happens? Those who have been in the business for a long time and have experience of acting in different situations have developed an awareness of the institutional variables. It is not uncommon for us to describe people like this as acting on intuition, or on their gut feelings. They have a sense of what works and are able to improvise solutions, but it is difficult to pinpoint exactly how they know this and what factors, based on their experience, they have taken into account.

For those who are convinced that the world is made up solely of clear, measurable connections, this is naturally problematic. Those with a more modest approach to the truth, however, see considerable explanatory value in it. When it comes to social conditions and circumstances, which are what characterize processes between organizations, and between individuals and organizations, there are many things that occur without us being able to observe or measure them. The point of departure here is that studies of clear, observable links between, for example, a buyer and a seller, an organization and a financier, or between a leader and the led, offer only limited explanations as to how organizations develop and why they do it in a particular way. Certainly such studies explain some conditions, such as who does what, for example; but we also need to know how social mechanisms work and why a certain development occurs in the manner it does. In order to grasp these difficult questions, we must look deeper – that is, beyond the obvious and directly observable, and delve beneath the surface in an attempt to see what is not visible with the naked eye. Those who live and work in different environments learn over time which invisible structures apply for the business they are involved in, making these structures very tangible for them and for the business conducted in the organizations they belong to. Often it is a matter of indirect influence, such as through the existence of general rules for a particular industry, laws, or that certain discourses (that is, ways of talking), paradigms (ways of thinking) and norms (ways of doing things) have become established around particular businesses, phenomena and fields.

An important point I intend to highlight is that elements in the institutional environment do not simply appear on their own. Thus they are by nature not a given, but their existence is a result of actors in the environment producing them, spreading them, and safeguarding them. This also means that how they are formed can be actively influenced, but, since it is a matter of a social interplay involving many actors, it is not easy to do. The book will provide insight into how elements in the institutional environment are created and thus show what processes it is important to be a part of if one wants to be involved and influence their direction.

The arguments presented in this book have thus been selected with an end to specifying the practical content of the institutional environment of organizations. The theoretical concept of the 'institutional environment' has been chosen because it expresses factors that have received too little attention in general discussions on why organizations develop the way they do. One thought with this book is that those who cultivate a better understanding of the factors included in the concept have the potential to encourage more actors not only to understand their role as actors in the market better, but also to make better choices.

The remainder of this chapter will be used to develop the book's starting point and present an outline of the rest of the book.

The starting point: organizations and environment

An underlying thought in the above discussion is that organizations are closely connected to what goes on in the world around them. The circumstances depicted until now, however, are not those usually in focus when discussing how organizations develop and change. We often hear that organizations are run by their managers and that organizing is something that should be viewed more as an instrument which management has at its disposal to lead the organization toward set goals. However, this picture is complicated by the fact that organizations, and here especially the organization in the form of a company, are assumed to compete in markets. Thus, all of the power is not assumed to lie in the hands of management, since the market also has an impact on what individual organizations can do and how they develop. Here, however, research in organization and marketing since the early 1980s has highlighted that companies are linked in different ways to a number of other actors around them. It has been argued, for example, that the network of financiers, suppliers and buyers they have direct exchanges with – an organization's 'stakeholders', as they are also called – places a number of demands on them. In organization studies, the most prominent genre that has drawn attention to these types of relationships is called 'industrial marketing' or 'network theory'. That organizations are connected to one another through different types of exchanges (where someone manufactures, someone buys, someone transports, someone finances, someone develops technology, etc.) is now a relatively widespread understanding of how organizations work. There is also a fair amount of literature that argues that individual organizations have the ability to influence and direct the development of their networks. This literature has thus drawn attention to the fact that governance of an organization does not stop at its own boundaries, but extends beyond them into its networks with other organizations. However, although they are important and of great significance for how we understand the development of organizations, these explanations are based primarily on a dimension that can be called 'observable'. It is possible to observe what other organizations an organization has exchanges with.

This is important if we want to understand how organizations develop, and there is also a great deal of literature that draws attention to this. But organizations are not only governed by the observable.

This book deals with the less obvious, that which is more difficult to observe, and which therefore receives less attention in the public debate and in the literature that attains a wide distribution. This attention deficit, however, is not due to the knowledge being unimportant – nor, for that matter, is it unknown to decision-makers. Rather, it is the other way around. It is a matter of a kind of knowledge that we often perceive as implicit and perhaps simply self-evident, that we learn 'along the way', but that is usually difficult to specify and hence also difficult to pass on. This knowledge therefore often becomes inaccessible to anyone other than the initiated. In other words, knowledge about what is not obvious is difficult to pass on because we are unable to observe exactly how it relates to the development of organizations.

Thus, the focus in this book is on a dimension of the environment other than what we first encounter in the organization and marketing literature, a dimension that is sometimes referred to as the institutional environment. It should, however, be noted that the concept of institutional environment is used here in a pragmatic sense and as a label for the legal, social and mental structures that individual organizations are embedded in. This means that our focus is the elements in the environment surrounding organizations that determine what they can do, what they must do, and what they should do and how they should do it. It is thus a question of factors that create room for organizations to act. The concept of institutional environment has its theoretical home in the so-called 'new institutional organizational analysis', where it is a central concept.[2] This theoretical body has to do with how organizations are influenced by societal factors such as ideas, rules, fashions, knowledge, ideologies, norms, etc., as well as how these are created and disseminated between organizations and cultures. As with many central concepts in this theory, however, the focus has not been directed toward systematizing the meaning of a concept. Although Scott[3] dedicated much effort to refining arguments and concepts, there is still no established systematic conceptual investigation.[4] The ambition here has not been to do this once and for all, but instead to try to flesh out a number of central concepts used in the institutional organizational analysis. These concepts reflect important circumstances in organizations' environment that decision-makers and others need to understand. This enables them to better understand the underlying processes and mechanisms – things that are not directly observable or obvious to anyone other than those deeply involved – that drive organizations to develop in certain directions.

There are a number of phenomena in, and aspects of, organizations' surrounding environment that send signals to individual organizations and individuals in these organizations, about how things should be run, organized and managed, and what organizations and individuals should do. An important starting point in the argument is therefore that it is not only the management, owners or boards of organizations that control this. Another assumption is that the environment surrounding organizations consists of more than the other actors that an organization has business exchanges with – for example, suppliers and customers. Direct business relations are naturally an important dimension of an organization's world, but the legal, social and psychological environment in which these exchanges occur is equally important.

Organizing beyond management

The introductory argument above states that organizations are embedded, partly in direct business relations and partly in the institutional environment that provides the framework for both the business relationships and for the business area and organization's ability to develop in one direction or another. If we believe this, then we should be able to find key reasons to why individual organizations evolve the way they do in the forces outside the organizations, as well as outside the direct relationships they have with actors in their immediate surroundings. It has also been suggested that this does not exactly reflect the picture we get from the dominant literature in the field, which tends to stress that the fate of organizations lies in the hands of their managers! How, then, are we to understand the importance of management? Equally as radical as claiming that an organization's success or failure lies in the hands of its management would be to interpret the above reasoning the other way around: that is, as though everything were governed by external factors and hence that management plays only a marginal role in what happens! The argument here, however, is more nuanced than either of these interpretations. All collective activity, such as that in organizations, occurs through different kinds of interaction. It involves interaction – between individuals, between organizations, between organizations and rules, between ideas and organizations, between norms, standards and organizations, between leaders and the led, etc. Thus, it is not a question of either one variable or another, but of the scope an organization has to act being determined by the combined interaction between these types of variables.

'Useful' knowledge
The literature on how organizations work and evolve is, however, dominated by discussions about precisely that: the importance of management. Research that advocates models of how management should act for their organizations to be successful is generally viewed in the public debate as representing 'useful' knowledge. This is a question that organization researchers are often asked by CEOs, politicians, consultants and journalists – that is, by those who practise management in some form. CEOs want to learn better methods for governance and control, consultants want fresh new models that they can build their consultancy around, politicians want to know the keys to success so they can develop policies for growth, and journalists want to write about topics that

readers want to read about. They all want to know the direct practical applications of the knowledge conveyed.

The question of what knowledge about organization and management can be useful is important for societal development, but it is also very intricate. The answers may not necessarily be found where most of us look for them. Moreover, the same knowledge may not be useful for everyone in every context! Before we can even begin to have a serious discussion on the topic, we need to get to know the lie of the land. We need to know where to start, how to proceed, at what pace, and who to take with us. Only then, once we have a nuanced understanding of this, can we begin to decide which paths to take and which directions will take us where we want to go. The hope is that this book will provide readers with a good basis upon which to begin this journey. In the meantime, however, readers must content themselves with my claim that what on the surface appears so attractive may not always be very useful. It may well also turn out that we need both what is good and what is useful in order to thrive and move in a positive direction over the long term. Too much of a good thing may not be so good, and too much of the useful may not be good either!

Books that answer a resounding *Yes* to the question of whether organizations can be governed are appealing because they not only provide clear answers to complex problems, but also claim these answers to be applicable in practice. This type of literature often stresses how our attention and energy should be directed toward developing knowledge and methods of how organizations can be better governed.[5] There are also authors who maintain that it is immoral not to pursue better understandings of how organizations work and can be governed.[6] However, it is not only books that devote efforts to these questions. Advisers of different kinds have also taken upon themselves the task of offering advice to management about how their organizations can be governed better. Separate organizations have also been formed for the purpose of developing international standards for better governance. The International Organization for Standardization is a good example, with quality and environmental standards (ISO 9000 and ISO 14000 series). Many organizational managers around the globe have also been assigned the responsibility of governing their respective organizations. For many of us, it is obvious that organizations can be governed and that it is management that does this. But does the mere fact that it has been established as a matter of course mean it is a reasonable explanation of how organizations evolve?

Organizations' managements naturally do a lot of things to steer organizations in a particular direction. Management is one force that affects how organizations evolve, but there are forces outside management that are also of importance, setting the framework or rules for what organizations and their managers can do. Perhaps the most talked-about force of this nature is the market. I will argue, however, that there are no 'natural' forces in markets and, rather, that in order to understand forces exerted by the market on individual organizations we must focus not only on market actors (that is, buyers and sellers) but also on what goes on outside the market (that is, in the institutional environment in which markets are embedded).

Beyond the market

An extensive amount of literature tones down the importance of management in favour of explanations stating that an organization's success or failure is determined by the market. However, this literature stresses the power and potential of 'economic man' – that is, a rational, profit-maximizing market actor who makes deliberate choices based on strategic analyses of how certain types of action lead to certain outcomes.

It is naturally important for all organizations that make a living by selling things that there are others to buy these things from them. Otherwise, they would soon cease to exist – that is, if there were no willing investors injecting new money all the time. Such was the case with many IT companies around the turn of the twenty-first century, for example, before the IT bubble burst.[7] The power of customers is important, and many organizations expend considerable effort adapting to customers' wishes. This often leads to interdependencies, however, especially in industrial contexts where a customer (Company A) may buy components from a supplier that are then used to make products sold on to its (Company A's) own customers. A chain of dependence is thus created, usually described as a network of relationships between organizations that are in various ways dependent on exchanges with each other.[8] This means, in addition, that customers adapt to what suppliers are able to supply. The power inherent in this mutual adaptation is strong and determines much of what is possible. Adapting to the market requires knowledge of which actors operate there, what their needs are, and what they produce. Such market relationships often also build on trust between the actors, and just as it takes time to build the trust needed for one organization to adapt its production to another – that is, to allow itself to become dependent on another organization – it often also takes time to absorb this trust. This means that relationships are often long-lived and are based on forces other than a buyer merely choosing the cheapest option. Often, customers would rather buy from someone they can count on, someone they have developed a trust for. It also means that, in practice, there is seldom an 'economic man'. It is rarely a matter of profit-maximization, but rather of security and social exchange and, consequently, of sufficient economic profit.

Managers and other individuals who have exchanges with other organizations are obviously able to influence the relationships their companies have with others. Their ability to act, however, is severely limited by the dependency that their organization has developed on other organizations. It is important to maintain trust and to continue to supply products and services that customers need. Any changes that the organization engages in must therefore occur in harmony with how the organizations it is bound to by business exchanges develop. The market thus limits management's ability to act. There are many who also claim that the market does not just limit an organization's ability to act, but also constitutes it. To some extent, this is naturally reasonable, at least if we direct our focus toward the direct exchanges organizations have with other organizations. However, it does not suffice as an explanation to how organizations evolve in certain directions. We must therefore look for explanations not only beyond what managers do and accomplish, but also beyond what occurs in the market and the forces found there. The collective term I use to describe this is 'the institutional environment'.

The institutional environment

The meaning of the concept of 'environment', as used in this book, is the world in which individual organizations are embedded. By 'embedded' I mean, as discussed above, the direct market relations which organizations have, as well as all of the indirect factors in the environment that limit organizations' and their managements' ability to act. The latter set of factors (the indirect ones) in particular, are those that are included here in the concept of the institutional environment. The question is then: what are they, and in what way do they constitute limits for what organizations can do? I defined the meaning briefly above, when I said that it was a matter of legal, social and mental structures.

Legal structures are the most tangible of these limits and also the most commonly referred to when discussing elements in the institutional environment. To look at a concrete example, the Swedish Companies Act stipulates, among other things, that all companies must have an auditor, a board, and a managing director. It also states that they must have a certain amount of capital, and that the ratio between this and any company debt must exceed a certain level in order that the company is not forced to draw up a balance sheet for possible liquidation. There are certainly options to choose from according to Swedish law for people who want to operate a business, in the form of a limited company, or sole proprietorship, partnership or limited partnership. Depending on the structure chosen, specific laws stipulate the requirements that must be met. The example demonstrates that legislation is an important component of society, which limits the ability of individual persons and organizations to act; but legislation does not simply happen on its own. The body in society with the right to legislate is the state, meaning that government agencies responsible for making law concerning business – in particular the ministry of labour, the tax authorities, and the ministries of trade and finance – must also be included in this environment. This means that politicians and civil servants working in these ministries and authorities are also part of the environment that organizations are embedded in.

The picture becomes even more complex when we include the social structures. In fact, civil servants and politicians who make decisions on laws do not do so without being affected by one another. They do not sit alone in their offices and *make up* laws. Their work has, for example, a large international component, to adapt Swedish legislation to what the EU has decided shall apply to all EU member states. In addition, they often surround themselves with experts and advisers who are either active practitioners in the field that the legislation pertains to, or who work as consultants to actors in that field of practice. Thus, politicians and civil servants in other countries, as well as actors who consult and represent others, perhaps competing companies, are also part of an organization's institutional environment.

That is a very concrete example of one element of the environment that limits an organization's ability to act: a law. I used this example partly to show how important the environment beyond the market is for what occurs in individual organizations and partly to illustrate how extensive and complex it is. A law does not simply come into being. It has to be produced through a process that involves a wide variety of cooperating actors – both national and international, and both private and public. Note also that this is only one example of *one* law, the Companies Act, and that there are numerous laws, national and international, that organizations must comply with. There are environmental laws, competition laws, accounting laws, laws governing contracts and work environments, labour market laws, etc., that regulate the space in which organizations and their managements operate. And if organizations break these laws, they must pay the penalty in the form of fines, jail time, damages, or denial of permissions sought. Laws are thus a very tangible and hence also an easily-grasped part of the environment beyond the market. To some extent, laws help to regulate how actors in the market behave in their relationships with one another, but they also help to regulate how the actual formation of a business occurs. For example, if someone wishes to apply for a bank loan in order to operate a certain business, the business must first be registered with the proper authority according to the legal form in which it intends to operate (in the Swedish case this means as a proprietorship, partnership, limited partnership, limited company, or association). Failing this, the business is not considered a legal entity and cannot enter into contracts, as it is only 'persons' – individual or legal – who can enter into contracts.

Thus, when it comes to limiting organizations' ability to act, laws are fundamental, and because they are visible, compliance with them is also predictable. It is also easy to predict what will happen if a law is not followed. In certain cases, organizations may take a calculated risk – for example, by not complying with environmental laws or contract laws – and hope that they can negotiate their way out of sticky situations if they get caught. But the institutional environment consists not only of formally binding laws and the actors who produce them; there are also a number of other elements that we, from a formal standpoint, adapt to voluntarily. This can involve standards or norms whose content we more or less take for granted. Both types of elements fall under the part of the institutional environment that we can call 'mental' structures. The mental structures are difficult to illustrate and difficult for outside observers to see. Even those who are deeply involved in a business can have difficulty seeing them because they are often taken for granted and therefore perceived as natural in a given situation.

Ultimately, the institutional environment can be described as consisting of sets of rules that determine what is legally, socially and psychologically permissible. Depending on what type of institutional element we are talking about, it can be placed in one of these categories. Unlike laws, which fall under the category of 'legal', norms, which belong in the psychological ('mental') and social categories, are not expressed in text. They are instead a question of exhortations that are normalized or that some people attempt to normalize in the settings where certain organizations operate. And although norms cannot be made visible in the same way as laws, they can constitute sharper boundaries to organizations' ability to act. That one should not break the law, for example, is a strong norm. Anyone who does so is considered a criminal and someone we are wary of trusting. Being exposed as a lawbreaker can thus carry broader consequences than being forced to pay a fine. One may also risk one's legitimacy as a trusted actor in that one has not only broken the formal law, but also the norm that one should not break the law.

Laws fall under the category of legally binding rules because they are explicit, written, intended to apply to everyone, and are compulsory and thereby have sanctions attached to them. Norms are also binding; yet, from a formal standpoint, following them is voluntary. Unlike laws, they are mainly associated with mental and social structures. Norms can be described as expectations established in modern society of what individuals or organizations of different natures are supposed to do in particular situations and how they are to go about doing it. Examples of clear norms are that we expect the dentist not to be dressed as a clown when she examines our teeth, or the managing director of Ericsson not to be dressed in men's clothes if she is a woman, or in women's clothes if he is a man. We also expect companies to make a profit and the police to not haggle over prices before responding when people call to report a crime in progress. When it comes to people in management positions, we expect them to set a good example and to not be the first to embezzle money from the company's coffers or walk off with materials used in company activities to build their own house or to be used in some other private pursuit on the side. We expect salespeople to be courteous and socially competent, and to be knowledgeable about the products and services they sell. Although these represent examples of expectations, which from a formal standpoint any actor is free to meet or not, in practice it is extremely difficult to go against an established norm, at least if you want to be seen as a legitimate actor within your field.

Business exchanges are largely a matter of various actors having confidence in each other. In order for us to trust other actors to the point that we enter into business exchanges with them, we expect a certain predictability in their behaviour. For example, we prefer that they do not manufacture cars one day and then provide health-care the next, or that they do nuclear research one day, and make candies and sweets the next. We want to be sure that they have expertise in the business areas in which they operate. We also prefer to have a particular contact person in the organization we are doing business with so that the tone of our conversations is good. We also want to know that we can rely on them to deliver at the agreed-upon time and preferably also that we can go back to them at a later date if need be, since it costs time, money and energy to find new suppliers one can rely on. We also want them to be at the address they give us, want the telephone number they give us to be correct, want them to answer our letters and emails, and want them not to be involved in nefarious activities or organized crime. That is, most people would rather borrow money from a commercial bank than from the Hell's Angels. Most of us also prefer to get our drugs from the pharmacy rather than in back alleys or from some downtown pusher. We would probably also prefer to buy a used car from an established car dealer rather than 'Honest Harry'.

Thus, the expectations of other actors, and especially the expectations of actors who operate in the same setting and who are potential customers, financiers or suppliers, greatly limit an individual organization's ability to act. The above examples illustrate some very tangible expectations based on well-established norms of good business conduct and generally upstanding behaviour in society. Someone who breaks these norms makes it more difficult for others to see him or her as a legitimate actor – that is, as someone we can trust and whose behaviour demonstrates a certain desired predictability.

A model to understand organizing beyond management and market

Up until now, the argumentation suggests that isolating explanations of how organizations develop into individual types of phenomena, such as management or market forces, is problematic. These phenomena are naturally not unimportant, but there are forces beyond them that also contribute to organizing; and not only to the organization of market exchanges, but also in that the creation of boundaries for what is possible contributes to what individual organizations and their managements can and must do in order to exist.

I mentioned above that elements in the environment do not simply appear on their own – individuals and organizations formulate them, ensure that they are adhered to, and come up with sanctions when needed. In order for them to exist, social exchange is needed, and to enable elements like norms to be shared by many requires a systematization over time in this social exchange. Because all three categories of structures contribute to setting the boundaries for and thereby regulating the ability of organizations and their managements to act, it is important for us to understand the ways in which they do this and how they differ and complement one another. Legal, social and mental structures in the form of laws, standards and norms, as well as knowledge, restrict what a leader can do and how an organization can act. This means that they also help to control how individual organizations evolve. If we want to understand how organizations evolve, and why they evolve in a certain way, we must also understand the interaction between management and market forces on the one hand, and legal, social and mental structures in the environment on the other.

The aim of this book is to flesh out this institutional environment, the background being that the environment is not made up of 'naturally occurring', objective elements, but that the structures are socially constructed. This means that they are created by individuals and groups of individuals who interact. Figure 1.1 shows some of the key elements in the institutional environment. The idea is to illustrate that an organization's environment can be seen as consisting of different layers, which can be roughly divided into the *immediate institutional environment* and the *wider institutional environment*. The immediate institutional environment comprises the actors that organizations, and individuals who work for them, meet, along with information, rules and services produced by them. The wider institutional environment, on the other hand, stresses the longer term in the form of criteria that can be linked to movements and social trends.

Closest to the organization lies the observable: that which everyone can see – that is, the exchanges the organization has with other organizations. These can be in the form of business exchanges, or they can be of a different character, such as exchanges of a financial or stakeholder nature. The demands these actors place on individual organizations are very tangible: for example, customers want their goods and services delivered, suppliers want to be paid for the delivered goods or services, and financiers want to see a return on invested capital. This represents very tangible pressure on organizations to do certain things in certain ways. These actors can be seen as the institutional environment's last outpost – that is, the channels through which the outside environment's combined pressures materialize into something tangible for each and every organization. Behind and alongside such materializations, however, are many activities that create and add to the pressure on organizations expressed by this type of actor.

Beyond the exchanges, but still of an immediate or direct character, we find a layer consisting of institutional actors and their products. This can be a matter of fashions for various management techniques and organizational forms channelled to organizations – for example, via market exchanges with management consultants. It can also be a matter of standard-setting organizations that produce standards or authorities that produce regulations. The institutional products and thereby also the institutional actors can have an effect on what the exchanges an organization has with other organizations look like.

The institutional environment

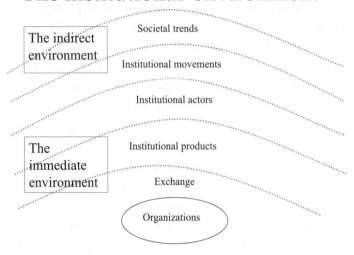

The indirect environment

Societal trends

Institutional movements

Institutional actors

The immediate environment

Institutional products

Exchange

Organizations

Figure 1.1   The institutional environment

Beyond the immediate environment, we find the more distant or indirect layers, such as movements and societal trends. In these layers, individual organizations do not need to be directly involved, but what happens here can nevertheless help to create, above all, mental structures, such as for what thoughts are legitimate to think in certain situations at certain times. For example, regulations and fashions are often clearly linked to various movements in society. 'Movements' here does not mean social movements where people gather in demonstrations and form barricades to protest something, like pollution, war, nuclear power, animal rights, the EU, or globalization. The reference is to more implicit movements, where large groups of people go about the same thing at about the same time in many places. An obvious example of such a movement is marketization. Public sector organizations and private companies around the world have, in recent decades, organized more and more as markets. They have sought to operate in a more business-like manner in order to become better market actors with clearer organizational forms, which are believed to be best suited for competing in markets. This does not occur in a vacuum, however, but can be associated with what we refer to here as the 'marketization movement'. This concept expresses the fact that a number of actors, operating at national and international levels, systematically, over a long period of time, advocate similar social forms of organization – in this case, the market. Examples of such actors include businesses and trade associations, government agencies, transnational government organizations such as the OECD, UN and WTO, as well as private organizations such as the International Organization for Standardization (ISO) and the European Organization for Quality (EOQ), and hybrid organizations such as, for example, the International Labour Organization (ILO), where governments, businesses and employees work together.

Most fundamental of all, however, is what can be called 'societal trends'. Here, I mean a certain direction in how we think about the development of society, a thinking that endures over time. In other words, societal trends characterize the fundamental way we look at how society is ordered. For the past 200 years, the dominating societal trend in the Western world has been modernity. To briefly touch upon the reasoning to come in Chapter 5, this means an approach in which we think in terms of making progress, that there must be growth, that we strive for predictability and calculability, that we should be able to measure and compare things, that we want order, and that we want to be able to control. The most distinctive feature of modernity is perhaps rationality – that is, in the sense that we look for a cause–effect relationship in almost everything we do. This fundamental way of thinking characterizes everything from politics to sports, enterprise and science, and also helps us to structure everyday events, such as justifying why we buy certain things or why we go to bed early the night before if we have a big day planned the following day. In a way, modernity is a complement to religion and social order. In the West, religion no longer holds the prominent position in society that it once did, and that it continues to hold in other parts of the world. In many countries, for example, Hinduism, Buddhism and Islam still have a significant impact on how society is organized. In Western countries, however, modernity has become the dominant societal trend.

In a way, the different types of elements can be seen as sediments of the environment that surrounds individual organizations. Figure 1.1 can therefore be likened to a hill. At the bottom of the hill is the individual organization. On top of this are the various layers of environmental elements that together represent very tangible pressure, which severely limits the organization's ability to act.

Conclusion and outline of the book

In this chapter, I have argued that neither management nor market forces suffice as explanations for why organizations develop as they do. To understand this development, we must look beyond the obvious, beyond the observable explanations, and try to understand the implicit mechanisms that drive both individuals and individual organizations in a certain direction. This book presents the argument that an understanding of the institutional environment is essential in this respect. It may not explain everything, but it can provide a valuable point of departure. This means that we need to know what makes up the institutional environment. In this chapter, a model that specified direct and indirect variables in the environment was developed. In Chapters 2 and 3, we will seek a more detailed understanding of the direct variables, represented here by *who the actors are* (producers of elements in the environment) and *what products they produce*. Following this, our attention in Chapters 4 and 5 will turn to the indirect variables *institutional movements* and *societal trends*. The book will then conclude with two chapters (6 and 7) on how the institutional environment influences organizations.

2. Institutional products

In this chapter, we will familiarize ourselves with the type of institutional environment elements that organizations encounter directly in everyday operations, namely elements that I refer to here as 'institutional products'. This includes materializations of knowledge, ideas and ideologies, such as those that individuals and organizations offer up to other individuals and organizations around the world. In this way, organizations encounter information, rules and services. In many cases, this involves services sold commercially, but it can also be a matter of information or regulations developed out of more general interests. What the two types have in common is that they are produced by one set of actors and directed at another. Thus, they contribute to the creation of legal, social and mental structures that organizations must adapt to in one way or another, and that consequently affect their ability to develop, what decisions can be made, and their options for governing and controlling organizations. They thereby also constitute the conditions necessary for organizations to be able to operate at all.

Institutional products can take many forms, and a crude division can be made into material products and social products, where the material products include information and rules, and the social products include services.

Also linked to the form institutional products take is how they are packaged. As with all types of products, products in the environment also need to be packaged. Two common forms of packaging are texts, such as reports and documents; and talk, in the form of presentations and discussions – that is, where the product is either written in the form of a regulation, or communicated by someone talking about it.

This chapter deals with the different characteristics these products may have. Figure 2.1 presents a list of the products focused on in this chapter.

Institutional products

- Materialized
  - Information
    - Ideas
    - Knowledge
    - Ideology

  - Rules
    - Standards
    - Codes
    - Directives

- Social
  - Services
    - Consultation
    - Education

Figure 2.1   Institutional products

Material products in the environment

The concept of 'material products' refers here to products that are materialized in a distributable form. Thus, we are talking about products that can be distributed to many people in the same format. Information and rules have been given a format that can be placed into someone's hands by being written down in a book or formalized as a rule. It is important to note that the categories used here represent a selection of rather broad categories. They can, however, be seen as covering most of the basic forms of material products that exist in the institutional environment surrounding organizations.

Information

The concept of 'information' is used here to depict the type of institutional products that do not belong to the category of 'rules'. This is not to say that information is a catch-all for anything that is not a rule. It is instead a question of two distinct categories of products, where one has the task of informing and the other of urging or exhorting.

The focus here is on information of a general character that is aimed at many people, often those other than the producers themselves. A clear tendency in recent decades has been for organizations to turn increasingly to other organizations to supply them with information they feel they have a need for. In order to be accessible – that is, to be spread from the person who has it or has acquired it – the information must be packaged in some way. Here, we distinguish between the form the information takes (its packaging) and its character. When it comes to the latter, this can involve packaged ideas, packaged knowledge, or packaged ideology.

It is thus a matter of information produced with the aim of informing other organizations and individuals about something specific, for example that a certain organization exists or that it has something specific to offer that could be of interest to others. However, it is also a matter of more general expressions of how organizations are believed to function, how they should be governed and controlled, how they can change or become more efficient, or how quality can be improved. Sometimes the information producers are very intent in their efforts to disseminate information and become very close to other organizations. One example of this is consulting. In such contexts, there may be information specifically produced for this particular organization. Often this involves information summarized in a report, which is only available to the organization that ordered it, in the form of either a document or a PowerPoint presentation.[9]

Knowledge

The ideal form of information is knowledge. Knowledge is an ideal because most people who disseminate information like to claim that the information represents just this. In everyday situations, knowledge claims are also linked to the fact that the information is about something that is true. Information presented as knowledge therefore has good potential to be perceived as believable, along with having good prospects of wide diffusion. In some contexts, for example, a book's author may claim that a book is believable because everything in it is based on personal experience. The author was there, and is telling about his or her own experiences, for example, of management. Other authors may claim that they visited so many organizations and gathered so much experience-based knowledge that they indeed know what they are talking about. As readers, however, it is difficult for us to verify whether the writer's conclusions are reasonable. We are left to judge the credibility of what is said based on whether we trust that the author really knows what he or she is talking about. It is also common for information producers to refer to the fact that they know more or less well-known people who have experienced things that attracted attention, or that they were involved in events that took place in large and perhaps internationally widely-spread organizations. Information producers may also refer to possible contacts in academia, where they may be invited to give guest lectures from time to time.

These methods of indicating that the producer of the information has a certain status are common for the type of information that attains wide diffusion. We can call this 'experience-based' knowledge. It may indeed be perfectly reasonable (that is, it may very well reflect how things actually are in the situations described by the author), but such information can hardly be seen as mobile, combinable or stable – attributes that are often used in science to classify whether the information produced should be deemed as representing knowledge.[10] If the author does not clearly explain the assumptions or open the arguments by discussing how the conclusions were reached, it is difficult for the discerning reader to combine these conclusions with those drawn by others, or with the reader's own experience or that of others around him or her. And since the construction of the conclusions is not presented, the information's stability can also be questioned. We cannot be sure that what is said is reasonable, either for the situations described or for other situations in other contexts. This can apply from one point in time to another within a single organization, or when comparing different organizations.

How we assess the mobility, combinability and stability of information can, however, have to do with whether or not we are confident that the author, with his or her experience, really knows what he or she is talking about. If we feel the author is credible in the circles we as readers or recipients of the information move in, we are likely to be less critical even if the rhetoric lacks clear references to and discussion of approaches and methods for choosing the information and analysis. However, this has to do with a text's social framework and not its isolated characteristics as a statement in itself.

Therefore, if a statement cannot be deemed mobile, combinable and stable, it should be classified as being of a different nature than knowledge. Note that I am speaking rhetorically here – that is, about the form of the expression and not about the practical relevance of the content. The point is to regard documents of various kinds as neutral from a social standpoint – that is, to see them as independent statements and to classify them as such. Statements that cannot be seen as mobile, combinable and stable, but where we must simply trust that the author knows what he or she is talking about, should therefore be characterized as something else. It is then a matter of one of the other forms of expression – that is, an idea or ideology. The form of expression is important because it can affect how we respond to it and handle its content. If we treat it as fact (truth), we put great faith in what is said and may use it as a basis for decisions and actions.

Ideology

When the demands for mobility, combinability and stability are not met, but there is still a systematic approach in the production of information, the information can be classified as ideology. It differs in form from knowledge foremost in limitations in the transparency of the reasoning. Ideology is undeniably also a matter of systematic thinking – that is, the ideas are linked and there are many who advocate the same thinking. However, the argumentation tends to be based on and built around certain ideas, beliefs or convictions, rather than open and combinable arguments. Either you believe the conclusions or you don't! There is, in reality, no in-between.

In the field of organization, there are a great many statements like this. They are often normative and contain proposed solutions to problems, often in the form of recommendations for ongoing improvements, better leadership, efficiency, better decision-making, etc. What remains characteristic is that the reasoning is based on an overall paradigmatic thinking. It is not a question of private ponderings or personal conviction, but of arguments that are stable in their context – that is, among the converted – but that are not open to combination or critique. Ideology is therefore often defined as specific sets of beliefs and ideas. Examples of ideologies that relate to organizations, entre-preneurship and management include neoliberalism in the form of free trade, competitive markets, and managerialism (that is, where certain forms of management and governance/control are seen as superior to other forms of decision-making).

Ideas

Ideas differ from knowledge and ideology in that ideas involve expressions that are less complex, where the systematization is less prominent and the starting points less visible. It is, however, still a matter of information because the aim is to express views for others to take note of. This may involve individuals or groups of individuals who advocate a view on how to achieve efficiency in organizations, or it may be about what characterizes successful management. The idea is often formulated as a concept – that is, a packaged solution with a specific label. The concept may be regarded as a tool used to achieve the intended effect. Examples of popular concepts/tools from the past three decades that can be mentioned are Business Culture, Quality Circles, TQM (Total Quality Management), BPR (Business Process Reengineering), BSC (Balanced Scorecard), Shareholder Value, and CSR (Corporate Social Responsibility).

Compared to the other categories of information – knowledge and ideology – ideas can be said to lack a wider social anchoring, at least to begin with. It is a matter of expressions that have distinct origins but that are not systematically confronted with other competing ideas as they are produced (that is, when they are formulated). As a rule, their formulation occurs within a limited circle, for example by individual people or smaller groups, as in networks or organizations. If ideas become popular, however, many others may then jump on board for a while, eagerly promoting a particular tool's excellence. In this case, though time-limited, there is a certain systematization.

Ideas can certainly be pushed hard, in the sense that proponents strongly advocate how fantastic an idea is or how good it would be for humankind, for particular organizations, or for the economy and the environment, if it were realized. Yet it is still a question of something fluid that we can either be for or against, or simply indifferent to. That is, we don't have to relate to an idea if no force is compelling us to. It is, however, not always the idea itself that bears this force. It can instead stem from the organizing that occurs around the idea, where various actors in various ways 'talk us into' the importance of these particular ideas over others. We will not go into this further now; but will content ourselves by noting that ideas are precisely the kind of information that many institutional environment actors produce.

Rules

All types of institutional environment elements can at times be seen as rules, though of varying character. In the most widely-spread institutional organizational analysis perspective, institutionalized notions of varying natures are seen as forming the ground-rules for certain phenomena in certain contexts.[11] They can then include psychological as well as legal and social exhortations. A more specific meaning of what rules are has been established in recent years, however, where the concept of 'rules' is associated with written exhortations intended for many people, and where there is most often a well-defined sanction system associated with the rules.[12] Unwritten exhortations can therefore be classified as norms (which is sometimes what we mean when we talk in general terms about unwritten rules). It is thus institutional environment elements that have to do with legal structures, or that strongly resemble such structures, that the term 'rules' aims to describe.

There are a lot of rules in the environment surrounding organizations – everything from tax laws to statutes governing the work of the boards of companies listed on the stock exchange. They are without a doubt materialized but, in contrast to information, in their exhortations, rules lay stricter claims on compliance. Rules exhort or urge. It is not simply a matter of a suggestion concerning what an organization *could* do; it is a matter of things that they *must* do. In this respect, however, there is a difference between rules that are compulsory, such as laws, and rules that are more voluntary, such as standards and codes. Everyone must follow laws if they want to avoid fines, imprisonment, or having permits withdrawn. With standards and codes, there is a formal option to choose whether or not to follow them. If you do choose to follow a standard, however, you also choose the sanction system attached to that standard. For example, if an organization opts to seek certification for its environmental work, and chooses to follow the guidelines set out in the ISO 14000 environmental management standard, it then also chooses the risk of not being granted certification because it does not meet the requirements, or having its certification revoked if it later fails to comply with the requirements of the standard. Standards and codes are thus very clear standard-setters in the surrounding environment with respect to how organizations should behave in order to be regarded as sufficiently legitimate in their context.

Directives

Directives are a special and very clear type of rules. In order for directives to exist, however, there must be a defined hierarchical system responsible for their formation and compliance. A directive is formulated by a superior and is meant to apply to subordinates in the particular context. Management is a ready-made example of this, where employees are expected to do what management decides. Directives are also binding and intended to impel others to carry out certain actions. There are therefore usually sanctions associated, for example, in the form of fines, imprisonment, reprimands or dismissal, when directives are not followed.

Although the practice of management can to some extent be seen as issuing directives, it is directives in the form of laws, official regulations and EU directives that we usually think of. Constitutions and laws are issued by government and ratified by parliament, while official regulations are issued by various government agencies. Although the principle is the same in all democracies around the world, it is likely to be national differences in practice. To illustrate how this can turn out in practice I use an example from Sweden. The following is an example of the way in which the Swedish National Road Administration (a Swedish authority) expresses how its regulations shall apply:[13]

> The government regulations that the National Road Administration decides on bind other government agencies, organizations and individuals to certain actions. In its operations, the Road Administration must accordingly also comply with regulations stipulated by other authorities in their respective areas of expertise.

Examples of regulations issued by the Road Administration include those relating to road markings, marking of resurfacing work, deviations from rules concerning the colour of road signs, etc. The Road Administration is not alone in this respect; most authorities issue regulations that apply within their area of responsibility. For example, the Swedish Work Environment Authority issues regulations regarding the use of forklifts, workplace noise, asbestos, systematic environmental work, workload, repetitive work, work on computer monitors, etc.

EU directives entail an obligation for the Swedish state to legislate or by other means ensure that the objectives of the directives are achieved. In contrast to national laws and the regulations of government agencies, EU directives apply to all member states, business operations and individuals included in the EU cooperation. An example is the EU's Machinery

Directive (MD 98/37/EC). The following is taken from the Swerea IVF website regarding the Machinery Directive, which entered into force on 1 January 1995:[14]

> As of today's date, the MD directive (98/37/EC) is mandatory. The directive deals with safety standards for the construction and manufacturing of new machinery and safety components, and can therefore be regarded as the machine manufacturer's rulebook. The aim is also to harmonize the laws of EEA countries (EU and EFTA), and the MD accordingly governs machine safety for the EEA market.
>
> There is also a Use of Work Equipment Directive (89/655/EEC) that serves as the machinery user's rulebook. This directive sets the requirements for the user's machinery, both new CE-certified machines and used non-CE-marked devices, which shall meet the applicable safety requirements.
>
> The MD directive (98/37/EC) applies to all companies that manufacture new machinery (including partly completed machinery). The directive gives provisions that manufacturers must apply in their construction so that machinery will be safe for users. Failing this, such machinery may not be put into operation by users in the European market. The regulations apply to both industry and consumer machinery.
>
> Because the majority of machines are electrically powered, the requirements of the Electromagnetic Compatibility Directive (89/336/EEC) and Low Voltage Directive (73/23/EEC) regarding electrical equipment for machinery apply. It is accordingly just pneumatically controlled machines that 'only' need to meet MD requirements. There are also other directives that may be applicable for certain equipment on/for machinery, such as ATEX (94/9/EC) for machinery used in potentially explosive atmospheres, the Simple Pressure Vessels Directive (87/404/EEC), the Pressure Equipment Directive (97/23/EC), etc.

The cited text shows that there are many EU directives which organizations in specific areas of activity must follow. It is important to note that this is just one example. There are EU directives about the handling of electronic waste, vehicles no longer in use, toy safety, marine equipment, elevators, etc.

It is certainly true that the final directives formulated and ratified are the result of special organizational processes – for example, of the ministries of finance, labour market and justice, Swedish Work Environment Authority, Swedish Competition Authority, EU Commission, etc. – but there is a complication here since governments, authorities and the EU act on a mandate from the people, the citizens. Formally, they are commissioned by the people. They issue directives because the voters give them the power to do so. The hierarchical system is thus a strategy by which to turn the will of the people into practical action. It is, however, special organizations that are responsible for this happening and for ensuring that the directives are followed.

To some degree, the processes in which directives are formulated resemble the processes in which standards are specified – that is, where the actors who de facto formulate directives or standards also act as representatives for broader interest groups. An important difference however is that, when it comes to directives, it is government or intergovernmental bodies (such as the EU) who are responsible for the processes, whereas the actors directly involved act on the voters' mandate and represent the will of the electorate.

To summarize, directives are like a written form of order. And, in practice, there is some kind of penalty for non-compliance. Directives are the result of processes and hierarchical systems and, here, there is a difference between an organization's internal directives and directives that apply to an entire area of activity in the EU, for example. In the case of the former, it is management that decides how the directives are to be formulated, and they are issued primarily to serve the interests of the owners of the organization. In the case of the latter, it is indeed individual organizations that formulate the directives, but they do so, formally, on behalf of the citizens.

Standards

A standard is also an exhortation but, as opposed to a directive, following or not following a standard is voluntary. There are sanction systems, but here it is not a question of the government collecting fines or handing out prison sentences through the legal system. Rather, it is a matter of revoking certification or not granting it in the first place. Standards are written and aimed at many people or organizations, and especially at those other than the ones who formulate them.

The ISO 9000 international quality management standard is a typical example of a standard for organizations, but the ISO also issues standards for areas such as environmental management (ISO 14000), and in 2008 launched a new standard for social responsibility (ISO 26000). But standards also occur in less formalized forms. Organizational fashions, such as

TQM (Total Quality Management) or BPR (Business Process Reengineering), can be regarded as standards, though there are no official sanctions associated with them other than people's propensity to give the organization in question legitimacy through a demand for its goods and services, or recommending them to others, etc. That is, there are indirect sanctions also for less formalized standards.

Codes

A special and growing type of standards are codes. Codes exist in a series of different contexts. The classical form is ethical codes for professionals. These codes are also the most visible because, as a rule, they are written down as requirements for membership of an association. The ethical codes for lawyers who belong to the Swedish Bar Association, for example, are clearly expressed. The same is true for doctors and the Swedish Medical Association, and for auditors who are members of the professional institute for certified accountants in Sweden (FAR). Anyone who breaks these codes or fails to meet the membership requirements will receive a reprimand, be thrown out, or not be considered for membership in the first place.

There is, however, a new type of code emerging. In recent years, for example, codes for social responsibility have begun to be developed. The UN is one of the organizations behind this, and the aim is for companies to take more social responsibility in relation to their employees, bringing to light morally questionable working conditions, such as child labour, the production of tobacco, alcohol and drugs, the manufacture of arms and munitions, etc. Banks might offer investors the option of saving their money in ethical funds. A hallmark of these types of funds is that they follow certain investment codes – that is, where they only invest in securities that cannot be linked to ethically dubious activities.

Codes are also found in other contexts. In Sweden, for example, at the beginning of the 2000s a great deal of energy was directed toward developing a code for corporate governance. The Swedish code has a form strongly reminiscent of similar codes in a number of EU countries. It builds to a large degree on the UK equivalent, the British Code for Corporate Governance.[15] The idea is that the composition of corporate boards and the responsibility they have should be equivalent in all publicly-traded companies worldwide to facilitate comparison and make it easier for investors and other owners to trust the boards who work for them.

Social products: services

Not every type of product that exists in the institutional environment of organizations is materialized in text format. In many cases, products take the form of services. Here, I am thinking primarily of education, consulting and investigations.

Education

Education takes different forms and can be found in compulsory and secondary schools, post-secondary education, at colleges and universities, and in various executive education programs offered by both academic institutions and independent non-academic bodies (such as consulting firms). Depending on who provides it, education can be configured differently. This also applies to the intended target group of the education. For students in academia, education usually involves lengthy courses with a heavy workload, while for employees of companies and public organizations attending various types of executive programs it generally involves shorter courses with lighter workloads. Variation does occur, however, under labels like *Full-time MBA* or *Executive MBA*, or diploma courses at institutions like IHM Business School, the Institute of Business Administration (FEI), IBS, etc. In these contexts, the education involves longer courses requiring a high work input from participants. In other contexts, it may be a matter of the participants gathering a few days a month for 6 months or so and, during this time, attending a number of lectures as well as hands-on work with other tasks. The time between these sessions, however, seldom involves assignments that have to be completed. Unlike MBAs and diploma programs, there are no degrees, even if a certificate or diploma may be issued to show participants attended the course.

In contexts where education is produced and delivered, many impressions about organizing, management, entrepreneurship, etc., are transmitted. Education is thus an important component in the environment of organizations. Organizations recruit people who have completed academic educations, and they send their own employees to various forms of executive education. One way organizations receive general knowledge on how organizations and organizational functions in the environment work is thus through recruiting educated individuals and through continuing education of existing employees.

Consulting

Consulting, or advisory services, is another form of service through which organizations find out about products in the surrounding environment. The most tangible category of actors who provide this service is naturally consultants, but there are others who provide organizations and individuals with advice in different contexts. For example, it is not unusual for some actors to occasionally act in a consulting role, despite their regular work being of a different nature. The World Bank, for example, may advise nations about how to increase their chances of receiving or renewing their loans. EU bodies may also offer advice to countries seeking entrance to the Union, with respect to how they should act in order to fulfil membership requirements. In such cases, the advice is clearly linked to well-defined and established requirements. Perhaps the most common form of advice not provided by specialized consultants, however, is that which is given on a daily basis between individuals engaged in exchanges of various characters. This may involve advice between colleagues, business acquaintances, friends and others who are part of different social networks.

The fact that managers of organizations surround themselves with advisers is a phenomenon that dates back a long way. Powerful men and women have more or less always used advisers to inform them of relevant and important occurrences in the domains they rule or are responsible for. One of history's most renowned advisers is probably Niccolo Machiavelli, who acted as an adviser to Florentine rulers in the late fifteenth and early sixteenth centuries. It is a matter of decision-makers wanting to surround themselves with a staff of advisers, preferably with different areas of specialty. Today, these advisers may be department or area managers employed in the organization, in charge of areas such as finance, sales or technical development, or people responsible for analysis, assessments, etc. The latter represent a category of advisers who have at times tended to be directly employed in the organizations they advise, and at other times been brought in mainly as external experts. Since the 1990s, for example, the latter form has been more common, where advisers have to a greater extent come from outside organizations and been called in when necessary. Prior to this, it was more common for people with these jobs to be employed internally in organizations.

When it comes to the hiring of outside advisers, there is often a certain systematization, since, if they perform well, the same consultants tend to be brought in repeatedly by the same companies. As a rule, however, the assignments are of a time-limited nature because one of the points of hiring an outside consultant is precisely that the consultant is external and, ideally, comes with other perspectives on things than employees would. It is important to note that there are many variations in how external consultants are hired, both when it comes to the content of their services and to the regularity and length of assignments. The idea here, however, is not to provide an exhaustive list of all forms of advisory services, but instead to provide a picture of how consultation occurs as a social product, a service, in the environment surrounding organizations.[16]

Investigation

Another type of service is investigation. Investigations are not performed for educational purposes, or in order to deliver advice, but in order to find out the current state of things. This may involve investigating different aspects of the national economy or industry, such as investigations by the Research Institute of Industrial Economics (IFN), but can also involve hiring consultants to investigate certain conditions – for example, how the work environment is perceived by the employees of an organization – or to conduct a market survey – that is, to investigate the market position of a specific organization and its products or services. It can also involve investigating financial flows, cost levels, or special investigations in an organization to find out what an investment would cost, or what kind of revenues it could bring.

Investigations are also common in politics to generate facts and a basis for making decisions on various issues. This can involve everything from power relationships in society or public sector administration, to more specific issues such as the accountability of the Swedish government, particular authorities and individuals in the 2004 Thai tsunami disaster.

Regardless of the type of investigation, the fundamental character of this form of service, investigation, differs from education and consultation. That consulting may be preceded by an investigation is another matter. In other words, it is not unusual for different types of services to be performed by one and the same category of actor. Consultants, for example, may well engage in both education and investigative activities. What is interesting here, however, is to note the variety of service types in the institutional environment of organizations, and that they can have different characters and affect organizations in different ways.

Packaging of institutional products: text and talk

Institutional products can be divided into the categories of *material* and *social*, and from there into the subcategories of *information*, *rules* and *services*. In practice, however, it is the packaging of these products that organizations and individuals encounter, though this does not make classifications of the content any less important. If we want to understand what the institutional environment consists of – that is, what it is that creates and maintains the structures in society that control us – it is important to break the environment down into its constituent parts and discuss the importance of the nature of the content and packaging. Doing this improves our chances of making more conscious choices about how we relate to various forms of demands from the institutional environment.

It is the packaging that organizations order and purchase. The packaging is also the form that institutional environment products are delivered in. Different types of products in the environment tend to be packaged in different ways.

When it comes to information of varying nature and rules, they are primarily disseminated in the form of text. It is common for information to be materialized, for example, in reports, documents, books or articles. Services, on the other hand, are characterized by talk, meaning that the content is disseminated orally in the form it is produced – that is, as education of different types, as consulting, or as the presentation of an investigation. However, the content of textualized information and rules can also be used in the service delivery, and thereby also constitute a step in the dissemination of content through talk. We can nevertheless make this distinction between text and talk, because the text can be said to have spread to the talk first. However, we must remain open to the fact that – in certain contexts – information is never textualized and only spreads via talk. Examples here include local discussions following education, a presentation, or when one or more people discuss a book or article they have read. In situations like this, a certain content is spread via talk.

Below, I will go through a few different forms of text found in the environment surrounding organizations and what distinguishes them. A discussion of different forms of talk follows.

Text as packaging

Packaging information in the form of a report is common. A report is characterized by someone having investigated something and written down their observations. Depending on the context in which the report is produced and used, it can be classified as representing scientific knowledge, experience-based knowledge, or ideology. If scientists are behind the report (which is not uncommon), it is expected to represent scientific knowledge. If it is practitioners – for example, managers of different operations working within the framework of a commissioned assignment – the report is expected to represent more experience-based knowledge. If consultants were hired to conduct an investigation and produce a report, the expectation may be that it will represent a combination of what can be classified as practical, relevant scientific knowledge and knowledge that builds on experience.

Thus, the context in which a report is produced and used has an impact on its eventual shape. As a rule, there are differences in how analyses are carried out, how conclusions are drawn, and the argumentation style used, between reports produced for scientific discussion, and those produced for use in political contexts where the primary purpose is to build opinion.

So, reports can differ. For example, various investigative bodies have taken it upon themselves to
produce reports in their special areas to inform
decision-makers in society. In Sweden, the Research
Institute of Industrial Economics (INF) produces information on conditions in industry, entrepreneurship and
economic trends. The National Institute of Economic
Research produces similar information but with a more
obvious focus on economic trends. The National
Labour Market Board (AMS) produces information on
labour market development, the National Agency for
Education in the area of education, the National
Agency for Higher Education on post-secondary education, the Nuclear Fuel and Waste Management Company (SKB) on conditions concerning nuclear power
as a source of energy, the National Food Agency on
food and food safety, the National Institute of Public
Health (FHI) and National Board of Health and Welfare on conditions relating to medical and health care,
disability, etc. There are also organizations that clearly
represent special interests, which also produce and
refer to reports of various kinds. Examples of such
organizations include the Confederation of Swedish
Enterprise, which represents the interests of employ-
ers, various labour organizations, such as the Swedish
Trade Union Confederation (LO), which represents the
interests of workers, and the Confederation of Professional Employees (TCO), which represents the interests of professional workers. These particular interest
groups all produce reports that have to do with issues
like economic and labour market trends, and their

reports are naturally also involved, along with organizations like the Institute of Economic Research and AMS, in shaping both public opinion, and labour market and economic policy. Producers of reports like these are key central actors, but they do not produce the reports in an information or interest vacuum. A series of different actors and interests is involved in the production process. Everyone involved contributes to the process, with information that they produced themselves, or information produced by others that they wish to communicate. Actors can also be specially assigned to drive certain issues – or not. SKB, for example, is not tasked with being anti-nuclear energy. Rather, its task is formulated as an express responsibility 'to manage and dispose of spent nuclear fuel and radioactive waste from Swedish nuclear power plants in such a way as to protect human health and the environment in the short and long term.'[17] Nor can AMS be expected to be opposed to labour market measures, or LO to union activities and employee influence in organizations. And nor can political parties be expected to be against the ideologies that they advocate.

There are also actors – for example, consultants – with a strong economic interest in conveying certain ideas. This information, and the reports that these types of organizations produce and refer to, can therefore be expected to represent thinking that underpins an organization's tasks and the interests the organization represents. The activities of these actors include the production of information, and the information they produce has a major impact. It is not unusual for reports on various topics to be used in the drafting of specific policies and as support for or opposition to different political opinions. Reports can also be used in the development of public sector activities of a more everyday nature, for example as a basis for decisions or in work on formulating rules and guidelines. They can also be used as a basis for organizational change and strategy development.

In order for a product in the environment to be considered a rule, it must be written. This is achieved through its publication in the form of a document. A document is thus a text with specific content. When it comes to information and rules produced in the public interest, a distinction can be made between a report and a document. A report is more comprehensive and can comprise the results of an investigation. It can then constitute the basis for producing specific documents. Documents are shorter texts and often contain decisions, strategies, exhortations, or notes from meetings, etc. Examples of regulatory documents are laws, standards and codes. In addition to regulatory documents, there are a number of other types of documents, such as minutes from board meetings, bases for decisions, policies, quality reports, administrative reports, financial statements, or strategic documents like plans, visions and budgets. It can also be a question of correspondence or memoranda. As a rule, these are intended for internal use only, but there are contexts in which they are published and therefore constitute elements in other organizations' institutional environment. In the case of public organizations, all of this material is public in that public sector organizations are governed by the access-to-information principle.

Talk as packaging

I discussed above how some services, such as investigations and certain forms of consulting, result in reports, while others, such as education and advice, never take this form. The latter can only be delivered in a social exchange between the service provider and the service recipient(s). Services must therefore be seen as a special form of distribution for certain institutional environment products.

Characteristic of services is that they only exist where they are performed. That is, they cannot be stored or textualized. They can obviously be described in texts ahead of time – that is, prior to delivery – and the delivery can be evaluated and documented afterwards, but the service itself only exists in what is commonly referred to as 'the moment of truth'.[18] Services can certainly also lead to texts – for example, investigations – but much of the process involves talk. Education is a typical example, where teachers talk in the form of lectures and where talk between participants occurs in seminars, etc. A lot of executive education in organizations involves precisely this: that participants assimilate the course material through talk. What happens is that actions are performed, and for the type of product in the environment focused on here, such as education and presentations, the action is talk. The form in which the information is conveyed is talk – that is, oral expressions are mediated. The specific content of what is said in different situations can naturally build on a variety of written sources, but the form in which it is mediated in the education, presentation or advice is talk.

Conclusion

In this chapter, I have specified the layer of the institutional environment surrounding organizations that I call 'institutional environment products'. A number of constituents of this layer have been discussed under the general categories of *material* and *social* products. This classification is made in an attempt to show that some products are materialized in texts of various kinds, such as reports and documents, while others occur only in social interaction between individuals, such as consulting and education. The form they take in this respect can be important when we assess how suitable they are and the practical relevance in the claims they make. A product that is left on its own, in the sense that it stands on its own in a text, has the potential to spread to many contexts. Examples of this are books sold by the million around the world, and international quality and environmental management standards that large numbers of organizations worldwide have been certified for. Figures show that in the case of the ISO 9000 quality standard alone, more than 600 000 organizations around the world have been certified! A product that is popular, that many people refer to, and that occurs in many contexts, has the potential to become an important starting point for many individuals and organizations as they form opinions about good and bad leadership, or good and bad organization. The products' suitability with respect to content may thus be secondary to the logic that, if so many people are doing it, it can't be wrong.

Social products may at the same time be quite convincing. A social product is delivered by one person to another. Depending on aspects such as authority relationships between these people, the information delivered can be perceived differently. If the person delivering the information is a well-established consultant with a good reputation, who may have written a number of popular books in the service's area of expertise, and the recipient is a younger manager in training, for example, it is likely that the consultant's words will carry a lot of weight. If the consultant is young and inexperienced and the recipient is a manager with extensive experience in the service's area of expertise, the reverse may be true.

We have also discussed how the products can represent different kinds of information. That is, they can be produced with different types of information as an underlying basis. This can involve knowledge, ideology or ideas. What a product is based on is important for what we do with the product once we acquire it. If it builds on knowledge, it has a stability, mobility and combinability that makes it specific and both controllable and usable in specific contexts. If, instead, it builds on ideology, its utility may be based on other grounds – that is, believing in something and sharing this belief with others can be very powerful. If the product builds more on ideas, these can serve as input in local processes of organizations. The latter is naturally something that all types of information can lead to. Also of importance is the packaging of products. If they are packaged in a text, they have been materialized, enabling them to be distributed to many. If, in addition, they have been validated through science (such as scientific reports), by government agencies (such as documents in the form of laws) or by international organizations like the ISO (standards), they have also been given the capacity to stand alone. They have thus been given various forms of accreditation in order to apply as reasonable facts. Although the form of an institutional product is important, how it is received may be a matter of how it is interpreted in the social context where it is received. The problematics of receiving and using information in different contexts will be discussed in Chapter 6.

3. Institutional actors

The trouble with the world is that the stupid are cocksure and the intelligent are full of doubt.

Bertrand Russell

Introduction

There are a great many actors in society whose main task is to encourage other actors to do certain things in a certain way. Governments and their agencies are obvious examples of this, as are supra- and inter-governmental organizations such as the EU and UN. Perhaps even more tangible an example are the consultants who offer advice and are involved in rule-making of various kinds; although there are also other actors like researchers, journalists, teachers, etc. What these 'institutional actors' have in common is that their work involves producing information, rules and services that will benefit other actors. They thereby summarize the requirements and conditions in society that apply for the rest of us. The information these actors convey can vary in character – as ideas, ideologies or knowledge – and they mediate it through either text or talk. That is, the activities and products of institutional environment actors contribute to the creation of both formal and informal structures in society that the rest of us (and sometimes they themselves) must relate to.

The production of institutional products clearly also involves many actors in various ways in various different contexts. The interest of this chapter, however, focuses mainly on those who can be said to make up the final link, thus the organizations that physically deliver institutional products to the organizations that consume them. When matters ultimately land on the desks of the actor categories discussed here, they are materialized in texts or packaged in talk.

Organizations among institutional actors

The activities of organizations are not only embedded in systems of the institutional products, but also in systems of the actors who produce and distribute the products. The question is: Who do we listen to amidst all the static in the world around us? Unfortunately, there is no obvious answer to this. It would be easy if there were a system that approved certain actors – that is, to ensure that the rules and information produced and represented by these actors were the best and most important. In some areas of expertise, such systems do exist. Here, I am thinking in particular of areas like medicine, law and auditing. The British philosopher Bertrand Russell says, however, that this may not be a wise strategy because there is no guarantee that those who most clearly indicate that they know what is good are actually the ones who really do know best. This is consistent with the image of practitioners and consultants on the one hand and academics on the other. Consultants would be those who present the definite answers, while academics often weigh things against each other and like to give alternative interpretations and answers, depending on different circumstances and assumptions. The most important answers may thus be found in the doubters, who perhaps do not deliver real answers but who are best at coming up with further questions. And while the answers of the uncertain may be the most right, as Barbara Czarniawska-Joerges suggests in a study of what management consultants do, it may just be that what is most wrong leads to the best actions.[19] That is, the content of a product in the environment, such as advice delivered by a management consultant, need not necessarily be correct. The important thing for the organization or individual receiving the advice may be what actions they take as a result of having received that advice.

However, I will not delve further into the benefits organizations reap from different elements in the institutional environment here, but will return to this discussion in Chapter 6. Here, our concentration is on the institutional actors and what characterizes them.

Organizations among information and rule producers

A number of actors in the environment in which organizations operate have opinions about *what* organizations should do and *how* they should do it. It is therefore not only customers who make such demands! Some actors also have the formal authority to force organizations to follow the rules set. Others are only able to try to persuade individual organizations that it is essential for them to put the actors' particular ideas to use. Regardless of what formal power they have, they place demands on organizations. And in some way or another, organizations must deal with these demands.

This means that, in addition to the actors that an individual or organization has various direct exchanges with (for example, financial, technical and logistic actors, or customers and suppliers), the environment surrounding organizations also houses a category of actors that the literature sometimes refers to as 'others'.[20] They are labelled 'others' because they often lack direct relations to individual organizations. Another peculiarity about them is that the activities they engage in are aimed at producing, packaging and distributing different expressions of how various phenomena in other organizations should work, or how various functions should be handled, and that they do not produce these for themselves. Their exhortations are primarily meant to apply to others. Their task can therefore be described as telling others how they could and should do things. I will give some examples of the kind of actors I am talking about here.

Among the UN and other 'others'
Perhaps the most notable actor in the 'others' category is the United Nations. What UN activities in general have to do with is the production of requirements for nations, not for the UN itself. For example, UN bodies tell nations at war that they should seek peace, but, if war nevertheless breaks out, they monitor the

respecting of human rights. They have established a special international court (the Hague Tribunal) for war crimes, and also operate a number of activities in addition to direct anti-war efforts, such as monitoring human rights and efforts to protect the environment around the world. This applies to both private life and work life, all in an aim to promote peaceful development on earth. The World Bank, for example, is an organization associated with the UN. It sets demands on nations to follow certain economic models with respect to social conditions in order to receive loans from the World Bank. The thought behind this is that certain models are better than others at promoting human rights and reducing the injustices of the world. The WTO (World Trade Organization) is another such organization, which works under the umbrella of the UN to develop forms for a functioning global trade, as this is assumed to reduce the risk of conflict and unnecessary environmental impact. The ILO (International Labour Organization) is also a UN organization, upon whose desk lies the work of monitoring labour trends so that human rights are taken into account in various types of work worldwide. An example is their fight against child labour. Children should instead be given the opportunity to go to school.

There are also many other organizations of this nature not connected to the UN. The OECD (Organisation for Economic Co-operation and Development) is one example. The OECD can be characterized as a meta-organization – that is, an organization whose members are other organizations. Its primary task is to produce information for the member countries' public administrations. It has, for example, been a strong advocate for the wave of reforms, commonly referred to as 'New Public Management', that public sector organizations in the West were subjected to mainly during the 1990s and first 5–6 years of the 2000s. In short, this entails that, where possible, the co-ordination of resources be achieved through market mechanisms rather than through hierarchy and bureaucracy.[21]

Another important actor of this calibre, whose operations affect many individuals and organizations in many countries, is the European Union. The EU invests considerable resources in harmonizing condi-tions between member states both for private citizens and for public administration and industry. It may thereby be seen mainly as a rule-producing actor, even if it is obviously also involved in information produc-tion, for example when it comes to providing infor-mation about which rules apply in different areas. The EU does this by harmonizing legislation between the member states and in other ways producing infor-mation and supporting standardization and the setting of norms. Hence, the idea is that special national regulations, which in certain local markets and in certain contexts are assumed to give some actors an advantage over others in the union, will be eliminated. For example, the EU works with competition-enhancing measures that level the playing field, so that individual actors do not have a monopoly, for example through acquisitions, in certain markets. From a Swedish viewpoint, we have observed this in

relation to merger attempts between truck manu-
facturers like Scania and Volvo, and Scania and Volks-
wagen, which were not permitted for competition
reasons. The EU has also drawn up a common standard for procurement procedures in public sector
organizations.

*Subcategories of 'others': individuals and
organizations*

'Others' can be divided further into different subcategories. Above, we briefly discussed 'others' that
can be defined as organizations, but 'others' may also
include individuals. Here, I am thinking of people
whose professional work involves producing and dis-
seminating information, participating in rule-making
in their capacity as experts of a specific field, and
being key service-providers. Examples of such actors
are consultants, researchers, teachers, politicians,
CEOs, and journalists. Through their operations, they
are also important in the construction of institutional
products.

The institutional environment actors can thus act as
individuals, but also as a collective in the form of
organizations like the UN, OECD, WTO and EU, trade
organizations such as Sweden's association for the
engineering industry (Teknikföretagen) or its association for electricity producers (Elproducentförbundet),
or interest groups like the Swedish Society for Nature
Conservation or Greenpeace, or non-governmental
organizations (NGOs) of different kinds. The products
they work with are mainly information, rules and

services. Idea producers often combine different forms of packaging. For example, it is common for consultants to write a book and give advice based on the book, and to be involved in rule production.

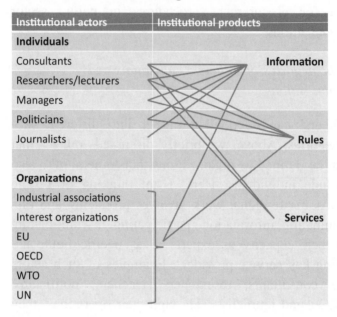

Figure 3.1   Institutional actors and their products

All of these actors operate around individual organizations. As illustrated in Figure 3.1, these actors can be divided into the categories of *rule producers*, *information producers* and *service producers*. Some types of actors – for example, consultants – can appear in several contexts.

Rule producers
Trade associations
Interest groups
EU, WTO, OECD, UN

Politicians
CEOs
Consultants

Information producers
Trade associations
Interest groups
EU, WTO, OECD, UN
Politicians
Researchers
Consultants
CEOs

Service producers
Teachers
Researchers
Consultants

Producers of rules, information and services
Both individuals and organizations produce information and rules about organizations and business
management. Consultants and researchers analyse the
organizations, write about them, and in this way
produce information on how organizations work, and
how they are led, managed and developed. Teachers
use such information in their teaching, in secondary
schools, colleges and universities, or in MBA and
other executive education programs.

There are also other organizations that produce
information. Trade associations, for example, have the
task of protecting a particular industry's interests in
different contexts. This often occurs by providing

politicians and civil servants at various government agencies with information that industry representatives want to be considered when things such as business, energy and labour market policy are drafted, as well as when rules are set in the form of international standards and legislation. They thereby serve as both information producers and as actors in rule-making processes.

However, trade associations may also produce ethical guidelines and professional norms that characterize representatives of their industry. They also help to create public images of companies that belong to the industry by speaking on behalf of the industry in the media, or endorsing books or advertising campaigns.

Another type of information producer is interest groups. Interest groups are formed to protect the interests of certain individuals or collectives. Those mentioned above are very clear examples: Greenpeace and the Swedish Society for Nature Conservation. Their task is to monitor environmental interests in the world and they try in different ways to encourage both individuals and organizations to protect the environment as much as possible. Another example of an interest organization is the Swedish Association for Quality. This organization is behind the production and monitoring of quality management standards in industry and public sector administration. Many countries have corresponding organizations and there is international cooperation via, for example, the European Foundation for Quality Management (EFQM) and the ISO.

There are, in addition, politicians and different types of national and international authorities, such as the Sweden's Agency for Economic and Regional Growth (Tillväxtverket) and the World Trade Organization (WTO). Tillväxtverket is a national agency in Sweden and many other countries have corresponding organizations. Their work involves evaluating and stimulating different branches of industry. The WTO is a kind of international agency, a so-called 'international governmental organization' (IGO) tasked with drawing up rules for trade and finance flows across national borders. The UN labour organization, ILO, is an organization of similar character, which monitors compliance with human rights in different areas of labour. The ILO is backed by three partners: industry, trade unions, and governments. It is the international cooperative body for national representatives of the three partners. A key issue for the ILO is to combat the exploitation of child labour in all countries around the world. Another issue with which the ILO works actively is the implementation of a model for entrepreneurship in the developing countries, as a method of combating unemployment among certain groups in certain regions.[22] It also monitors working conditions in various industries. One example of interest is its regular updates of a book presented as a guide to the profession of management consulting.[23]

The most tangible category of institutional environment actors for organizations is consultants. The main purpose of consultants' activities is to sell services to various organizations. If they do not succeed at this, they cannot work as consultants. They therefore move in proximity to organizations, regularly reminding potential clients of their presence in the hope that they will be hired. A typical consulting service is characterized by advice. Often this is provided using popular organization and leadership models as a starting point. In that consultants usually carry out assignments in many organizations, they contribute to the dissemination of specific models in society. US management consulting firms often run their businesses internationally and number among the 10–20 biggest companies in many countries.[24] As a rule, these firms are also behind globally distributed practically oriented handbooks in the areas of management and leadership. Consultants are therefore important contributors to the shaping of institutional information (ideas, knowledge, ideologies).

Although one key task is to give advice, management consulting also includes a number of other types of services. It is common that a distinction is made between expert consultants and process consultants, where the former are assumed to deliver complete solutions and are thereby the most important distributors of models, while the latter are assumed to begin by defining problems in individual organizations and then suggest solutions to fit particular situations.[25] But even this group tends to build its activities on popular information.

Empirical studies on the activities of management consultants show that their fields of endeavour are fairly broad, and that the categories of *expert consultant* and *process consultant* are also too broad. Using instead three categories – *external resources, intermediaries* and *supporters* – is more representative.[26] This means that consultants sometimes fulfil the function of providing the expertise that employees don't have, or of performing the tasks that employees don't have time for. This can involve the investigation, development and implementation of administrative systems, analysis of the work environment, market position, strategies for the future, etc. It can also be a question of them bringing with them knowledge and experience that they spread to organizations through education and implementation of management standards, codes, etc.

An important component of all of these functions is that consultants to a large extent build their services on popular information, which in many situations makes them implicit intermediaries of institutional products. But it can also be a matter of business coaching – that is, that consultants are there as a sounding board for management – or that they, by way of a series of interviews, give the workers in an organization an opportunity to voice their thoughts on matters such as working conditions, the future of the organization, etc., making employees feel as though they are being heard, and thereby enabling them to feel more motivated. In such contexts, they can be regarded more as actors in organizations' networks – that is, actors that organizations have direct business exchanges with. This means that it is mostly in other functions, when they are involved in rule and information production, and the dissemination of these, that they can be seen as institutional actors.

Conclusion

For organizations, it is the immediate environment that is the most tangible. It is the world they encounter every day. They have exchanges with other organizations and individuals, and they are surrounded by more or less explicit institutional products, and thereby also by the actors that produce and deliver them – that is, institutional actors. Immediate institutional actors create explicit structures that limit the organizations' ability to act. A good understanding of these structures creates opportunities for conscious direct action, even if it can be difficult to know which products and actors should be prioritized and how to relate to them, and in which situations different kinds of behaviour are suitable. However, a good understanding helps us to be prepared for situations that can arise. Organizations and their managers can also prepare themselves for alternative courses of action, the suitability of which may vary depending on the situation.

4. Institutional movements

From the immediate to the wider institutional environment

I will now move on to a discussion of elements in the wider, more indirect institutional environment of organizations. An important question is then where the line between indirect and direct elements can be drawn. Possibly such a division lends itself to be made analytically, but it is difficult to define precisely where the boundary lies in practice. We can, however, distinguish between actors and products, as I did in Chapters 2 and 3. We can also distinguish between the visible and what lies beneath, the silent and less easily visible.

In previous chapters, I discussed how such components in the institutional environment of organizations can be said to be directly linked to the activities of individual organizations. Individual organizations meet consultants, buy books, apply standards, must follow rules, etc. The immediate environment can therefore be described as more direct, visible and well-defined with respect to its structures. We are now moving from the direct dimension into the less obvious – that is, to those institutional environment elements that cannot be directly associated with particular actors or products. This does not mean that the wider institutional environment is less important to our understanding of why organizations evolve in a certain direction. Quite the opposite: the indirect dimension is highly significant, but it is not at all certain that individuals in organizations perceive that they are affected by it.

In the next two chapters, I will attempt to specify what this wider institutional environment is composed of. I begin here by discussing institutional movements and will discuss societal trends in Chapter 5.

Institutional movements as elements in the institutional environment

There is no question that social structures exist, but defining where one structure ends and another begins is not an easy task. We can draw certain boundaries, such as between different organizations. In one sense, organizations constitute social boundaries, but they are also interwoven with various personal and business relationships and, in that they are subject to the same information and regulatory framework, belong to the same overall contexts, such as an industry, sector, etc. One example is if one were to try to draw a sharp line between where acquaintanceship and collegiality end and friendship begins. These concepts express different types of social structures with respect to how strong they are. Being acquainted with someone is something more fleeting than friendship, and collegiality is generally more limited than friendship, while the latter can best be described as something unconditional and timeless. Another example is where we would draw the boundary between friendship and a business connection, or between people we know and trust and those who are more unreliable. Even if it is difficult to draw these lines, our belonging in different social contexts affects how we relate to other people and organizations, as well as to institutional actors and products.

By a 'movement' I mean here that many organizations at about the same time undertake similar measures, or endeavour to introduce similar organizational forms. To be able to classify something as a movement, however, also requires that it occur more or less simultaneously in many places. I am not referring to the classical meaning of a social movement here, where different types of actors of an interest group or ideology join forces to systematically drive a common issue. Examples of typical social movements are the environmental movement, the labour movement, and the peace movement. Such movements typically demonstrate clear links between different actor groups. Similar structures are built up in different places and there is a common organization. It is a matter of visible networks and may involve membership in interest organizations, such as Greenpeace.

The type of movement I am mainly thinking of here, however, is of a different nature. Certainly, there may be structures of the classical nature in the areas of management and organization as well, but here one rarely finds a large number of people with different backgrounds physically gathered around a common purpose or issue such as world peace or a healthier environment. Here, we do not see people demonstrating for 'more TQM in schools', or 'BPR for everyone'. It is hardly the issue itself that is the focus – that it would be better for humanity if more companies implemented management concepts like BPR or TQM, or Balanced Scorecard. Rather, if a large group of people join together in a more or less organized form, it is more likely that they do so because they see an element of personal gain in their engagement. There are, however, certain issues that engage large numbers in ways that resemble more traditional movements; but it is then a question of more fundamental issues with a strong ideological base, which are also linked to society's development in general.[27] For the past 20 years, it has been claimed in different contexts that we are seeing a number of very tangible movements like these in international society. We have seen them everywhere, in both the private and public sectors; we have seen them in many countries; but we have also seen that these movements express themselves in different ways in different contexts. The most evident, perhaps, were the movements for public sector organizations and associations. For those with previously distinct identities, such as government agencies, municipalities, hospitals, schools, public service corporations, sports clubs, etc., it is no longer enough for them to be seen as legitimate. Over the past 20 years, a series of ideologically-linked reforms has led to the establishment of a different approach. The idea that has unified most of these reforms is the autonomous company that competes in markets.[28]

One consequence of this trend is that different institutional starting points meet and blend together. Until the mid-1980s, what a 'school' was, for example, was unproblematic. If we take Sweden as an example, schools were placed in the areas where children lived. They had definite catchment areas and there was a fixed national curriculum that had to be followed by all schools across the country. The head of the school was the school principal, and every school was also part of a larger school district. These structures naturally still remain, but the responsibility of the school principal as the head of the school has changed. Today, he or she is head of a profit centre that competes in the school market where there are now also private alternatives run in the form of limited companies. This has resulted in every school being seen as an autonomous unit with its own identity, its own hierarchy, and its own rationality – that is, schools need to have their own goals, their own budgets and leaders who manage school operations, not just managers who administrate, and who are accountable for the results. In some cases, these managers are also owners of limited companies where schools are the business concept. Thus, they no longer have to live up to the institution of the school alone, but also to the institution of the organization. The goal is no longer simply to offer all children in the catchment area a good education, but also to satisfy those with an economic interest in the school's results, such as the owners and the customers (that is, the parents and children who 'buy' their education places).

The same applies to clubs and associations. It is now common that an increasing number of sports associations operate as limited companies. This becomes particularly evident the closer you get to elite levels. There, it is a question of an association's ever-increasing financial commitments that require a different way of thinking and acting than if the association is lower down in the divisions. For hockey teams in the Swedish First or Second League, or a football team in the Premiership or Super One, for example, there are also clear financial requirements for elite licensing by the Swedish Sports Confederation (RF). If a club plays at the elite level, it must meet the financial requirements; otherwise it will be forced to move down in the league system. Meeting athletic demands is self-regulating for teams in connection with their wins and losses in league play. The financial demands, on the other hand, must be managed by experts. Although the limited company is not always chosen as the form of association, even those who choose to continue to operate in the form of a club or association must do so through a practice that to all intents and purposes is business-like.

A similar development was seen in the Swedish savings banks movement.[29] The savings banks began as local savings branches for individuals, but during the 1980s in particular there was a strong drive for savings banks to abandon their origins and become more like the 'real' commercial banks, with SHB and SEB serving as the obvious examples. Right before the banking crisis in the early 1990s, I interviewed a management consultant who said that, in his consulting firm, the opinion was that Första Sparbanken (a savings bank) was Sweden's most innovative bank. This bank then became one of those that fared worst during that financial crisis, reaching the brink of bankruptcy and only surviving thanks to the creation of a national bank support agency (commonly known as 'Bankakuten').[30] The phenomenon of organizations of different characters that operate different activities (from football to banking) choosing, at around the same time, to structure and run their operations in a similar manner, is referred to here as an 'institutional movement'. These organizations march together, though not explicitly and not by bearing placards, shouting slogans, or practising civil disobedience, as seen in certain factions of the anti-globalization movement.

Below, I give examples of what some central movements for organizations involve and stand for. Following this is a discussion of how the movements are constructed – that is, how different actors come together and take part in a common, parallel, virtual demonstration around the world, through which special ideas take hold.

Examples of movements:

- Marketization
- Organization
- Corporatization
- Managementization
- Expertization

Marketization

In the 'movement' context, the ending *-ization* here describes something that is ongoing, and not something that merely happened at one specific point in time. Marketization may well be the strongest and most fundamental movement in the organizational world since the beginning of the 1980s. The ideas of coordinating and systematizing resources via markets, however, have been around much longer. One example is the work of the 1991 Nobel laureate in economics, Ronald Coase, who argued as early as 1937 that market solutions should be undertaken when the transaction costs of internal solutions, within hierarchies (firms), are higher. This was not a new idea at the time either, being reminiscent of Adam Smith's (1776 [2001]) arguments on comparative advantage – that is, that whoever can produce something at the lowest cost should produce it and, consequently, that things that cost more to produce yourself should be bought from others who can produce them for less.

The marketization movement in focus here clearly uses these fundamental ideas on market as a point of departure, but it is strongly linked, ideologically, to political contexts where market solutions are espoused. Even if it was not former UK prime minister Margaret Thatcher or US president Ronald Reagan who introduced the belief that market mechanisms are more effective than hierarchies when it comes to organizing public sector activities, it was early in their reigns, around 1980, that the systematic use of market solutions as a basis for reforming the public sectors of the Western world began.[31] Sweden, Canada and New Zealand were among the early adopters of these ideas. In Sweden this meant that state-owned companies were privatized, purchasing was to be subject to competition, and procurement and marketing reforms were introduced in health care and municipal operations where certain organizations were to act as the purchasers and others as the providers.[32] An important aim of the reforms was that both the purchasing and the providing should be carried out under competitive conditions, thereby creating the stimulus for both buyers and sellers to become more effective. The possibility should exist for the purchaser to buy from actors other than state or municipal providers if the latter were unable to deliver at more competitive prices. Many countries have implemented similar reforms since the late 1980s, and Sweden is no exception. An example of this is the drawing-up of guidelines for how public organizations should act in order to create competition in connection with purchasing, leading to the introduction of new legislation in 1994: the Public Procurement Act.[33] All of the countries in the EU have similar laws, meaning that all purchases over a specified value must be duly advertised so that everyone in the EU who wants to has the opportunity to submit a quote in connection with various procurements.

A consequence of marketization for citizens has been that they are expected to become customers in more contexts. For example, they are expected to demand health care as customers rather than citizens with a right to the best possible care, where the professional system is responsible for providing citizens with the health care they can foreseeably have a need for. Departments in hospitals have become individual profit centres and must buy and sell goods and services from and to one another.

Even in industry, market thinking has become increasingly important since the beginning of the 1980s. Examples of widely-used methods and concepts for increasing effectiveness in production and profitability are: internal pricing, accountability for results, process ownership, quality assurance, and competition. What, then, does it mean that we live in a time of ongoing marketization? There is a fundamental difference between the institution-citizen and the institution-customer.[34] A customer makes an active choice. A customer chooses between alternatives. A customer chooses that which offers the best value for the price and is most rational. A citizen receives the care that the hospital, or the education that the school, is able to offer. All citizens have the same right to the same health care or education regardless of where they live, what knowledge they have, or how much they are able to pay. That is, they do not need to choose because the democratic system guarantees that all health care and all education are equal and accessible for everyone. A customer, on the other hand, can choose a particular hospital, or doctor, or school, and is expected to compare the options available and the quality and prices on offer from different suppliers.

Marketization entails also that the citizen is now expected to be a customer. As a customer, we are able to choose our electricity supplier and our telephone supplier. We can choose to drive our car across a bridge or travel by boat, or choose whether to drive into the city and pay congestion taxes, or on certain highways, or to get to where we are going by other, cheaper means. We can also choose radio and TV programs from different channels, etc. In an increasing number of areas, we are thus expected to be customers, and we are expected to make rational choices about suppliers – that is, to not pay more than necessary and to choose the most advantageous alternative. Otherwise, we are not true customers, and the market does not work. We are therefore also expected to acquire the expertise needed to be able to make market-based decisions regarding things such as electricity, telecom operators, TV sets, radio channels, or pension funds.

What makes marketization a movement is that market solutions begin to be promoted and introduced in many places during the same period. Reagan's and Thatcher's regimes in the US and UK, respectively, did this at approximately the same time, despite not engaging in joint actions or solutions. Many other countries then followed suit. One of the later manifestations of marketization is the concept of New Public Management (NPM). NPM was launched as a concept in the middle of the 1990s in order to describe the market experiments being conducted for a number of years in some countries. New Zealand came to be the example that other countries wanted to copy. Delegations were sent there from other countries to study how they had succeeded in introducing market solutions in the public sector. The OECD later developed measures and ideas for how NPM could be realized in more countries.

Organization

Connected to the idea of a real market actor having to operate efficiently in the market is also the organization movement. In order to be a rational market actor (to be self-sufficient, effective, results-oriented and productive) a unit must become a 'real' organization. A real organization has a distinct identity and is autonomous – that is, it can be isolated from other activities. Real organizations therefore have goals, strategies, plans and business concepts. To be able to determine whether an organization fulfils these criteria, certain measures have also been developed. For example, the financial flow of an organization is reported in a certain way. This enables us to use special key values that are regarded as being able to show how efficient, productive, profitable and solid the organization is. An organization should thus be something that is separable, measurable, and manageable, something made up of controllable interconnected processes – that is, something very rational. Manageability and controllability also imply that there is a hierarchy – that is, a structure for how the organization is managed, and how responsibility and authority are divided.

Like marketization, organization can be seen as a fundamental movement, and the two are also closely linked. Marketization requires the existence of organizations, since markets consist of more than just individual buyers and sellers – they also consist of organizations that buy from and sell to each other. As discussed above, the idea is that when organizing represents a cheaper and more efficient solution than markets, resources should be allocated through organization, and vice versa when market solutions are thought to be more efficient. It can seem paradoxical to discuss the movements of marketization and organization parallel to one another, since they advocate two separate ways of structuring society, but essentially they go hand in hand and support one another. 'Real' organizations are perfect market actors!

Corporatization

The company, or corporation, is a special form of organization. The foundations are the same as for the organization movement – that is, that units must have an identity, a hierarchy and a rationality. But the company is even more precise. It must be self-sufficient, must generate a profit, and must be productive and competitive. Linked to the idea of market creation is the idea of the company as the central market actor. When the public sector attempts to distribute resources via markets, using variations of buy and sell systems, it usually also means that the organizations from which they buy and to which they sell begin to be seen as companies.

Privatization and incorporation are two typical examples of what is meant by corporatization. As the name suggests, 'privatization' deals with the sale of public sector activities to private interests, while incorporation can occur in both private industry and the public realm. In industry, corporatization has primarily been carried out under the guise of a focus on core activities. The concept represents a key component in management fashions such as BPR (Business Process Reengineering) and TQM (Total Quality Management), the idea being that activities should be divided up into processes. If this can be done through the formation of a company, then the responsibility for the various areas of activity becomes very clear. Another variation has been to create companies through the acquisition of other companies. But this also follows a number of requirements.

The company is the norm, where companies, like individual citizens, must 'buy' electricity, health care, schooling, elderly care, etc., as real market actors. The customer is one type of market actor, the other being the supplier. If organizations are to operate in markets, they must also act as companies. The institution of market thus implies that both the institution of customer and the institution of company are adhered to. The marketization movement – that is, where we try to create market situations in more and more areas – brings with it the corporatization movement.

Managementization

The organization movement entails a demand that units have a hierarchy – that is, a distinct chain of command. This became even clearer above, in our discussion of the corporatization movement. Real organizations have CEOs, who are assumed to lead and manage the organizations they have managerial responsibility for. This means that we can talk about yet another parallel movement, namely management-ization. As the number of activities that begin to be seen as organizations or companies grows, the more managers we get, because all organizations and companies must have a clear chain of command. There is also legislation stipulating that companies have a managing director and a board that these managers report to.

This implies that certain people – that is, managers – are given the responsibility of showing acceptable results for the processes they manage. This thinking is not new. In SHB (a Swedish commercial bank), for example, it has been an underlying concept for branch operations since the early 1970s. If a branch fails to show satisfactory financial results, the branch manager is replaced. The reverse has also occurred – that is, that if a branch is doing really well, the branch manager is readily dispatched to new and greater challenges. What is new, especially in the public sector, is that civil servants and administrative directors or director generals are increasingly regarded as managers. They are no longer 'merely' heads of an authority, such as the National Road Administration for example, but must behave as CEOs running a business in competition, acting as if they were managers of a company. This is even more obvious in contexts where privatization and corporatization have occurred. There is a big difference between what is expected of the managing director or CEO of the corporatized Telia Sonera (a Swedish/Finnish telecom firm) and the expectations we had in Sweden of the director general of its predecessor Televerket, the former national telecom agency.

Following on from greater expectations for organizations to have managers are greater demands on our ability to measure their performance. The most common thinking here is that an organization's results are a measure of the leader's performance. A number of methods for measuring the results of organizations have therefore been developed. Economic measures are one example, but there are also other measures such as ratings, rankings, quality assessment points, and certification.

Today, there are many positions in companies sporting the title of 'manager', and special courses in business management are offered at both post-secondary institutions and consulting firms. And even though you work for a Swedish company, you may well be given an English title like *area manager* or *account manager*, etc. By definition, organizations have managers, and real organizations operate like companies, and thus have CEOs, regardless of what their responsibilities are. Even the director of a public hospital must serve as a CEO. For example, in the middle of the 1990s, Karolinska University Hospital in Stockholm recruited as its director a physician and doctor of medicine with experience of management positions in the pharmaceutical industry. An increasingly important criterion in the appointment of vice chancellors of universities is that they also have good business leadership qualities. School principals are increasingly called 'school managers'. Privatization and corporatization have led to the restructuring of authorities as companies and they have been given managing directors instead of directors general. Sports clubs and associations have also been given managing directors in place of chairmen, and executive groups in place of boards, etc.

The debate about how the public sector should be made more efficient has to a large extent to do with management – that is, that 'real' leaders who think like business managers must be recruited.[35] The 'ugly sister' must be made over and dressed in business management techniques.[36] The public sector must implement market models never before used in practice, and become more like the institution of a company than private companies ever were.[37] In the late 1990s, the movements discussed here began to be brought together under the concept of new public management, where the emphasis was on management rather than administration.[38]

Expertization

If marketization, organization, corporatization and managementization can be seen as four parallel and cooperating movements, the expertization movement differs somewhat from the rest. On one level, however, it is well in line with marketization. Expertization can be likened to a modern variant of Adam Smith's ideas on comparative advantage and Coase's transaction cost theory. That is, the one who is best placed and best equipped to achieve good results in an efficient manner is also the one who should do the job. If this happens to be someone other than oneself, then one should buy the service from the other person, or possibly trade services if this is an option.

The fundamental idea of the expertization movement is that today's society is so complex that specialists are required in a growing number of areas to manage different tasks and matters efficiently.[39] Over time, more or less advanced systems develop around some of these specialized tasks. These we can call 'expert systems', where status systems for different categories of experts are constructed. For example, an association for professional experts may be created. Examples of such systems in Sweden include FAR (the professional institute for certified public accountants), the Swedish Bar Association and the Swedish Medical Association. As a rule, these associations then have special requirements that those seeking membership must meet. The requirements are usually materialized in the form of special rules regarding education and experience.

Since the early 1990s, it has become increasingly common for organizations to let go of certain work tasks in the belief they can be carried out more efficiently by others. *Outsourcing* was a popular name for this in the first decade of the twenty-first century. Processes and work tasks that are not judged to belong to core activities have been externalized – that is, moved out of the organization to the market. This means that they are carried out by market actors rather than organization members. They can involve everything from routinized manufacturing, administration and reception services, to pure specialist tasks, such as analysis, evaluation, strategy work, management development or organizational development, that organizations do not have a daily need for but cannot manage without. An important idea has been that organizations should not have to pay more than necessary for this extra capacity. One requirement for being able to call in external experts and specialists from the outside when needed, however, is that the tasks they will be working on should be standardized to some extent, so that they can quickly jump in and do work that is relevant.

Flexibility is a concept that during the first decade of the twenty-first century in particular has been used as a key argument for why organizations should concentrate on core activities and maintain as small a 'core' as possible. The idea has been that organizations should be prepared to rapidly adapt to changes in the surrounding environment and not be locked into costly investments with respect to real estate, machinery, inventory and obligations to employees. A cause of concern for many organizations has been increased internationalization, for example by way of the EU's internal market and the elimination of trade barriers (WTO). Such a development is assumed to lead to stiffer international competition on more markets, as well as to changes in institutional conditions.

During the 1960s and 1970s, the dominating idea was that risk should be spread – that we shouldn't put all our eggs in one basket. Many larger companies therefore developed into conglomerates – that is, to enable them to operate widely varying activities within the framework of one concern. The Swedish car manufacturer Volvo, for example, was active in the automobile, food and pharmaceutical industries. The logic was that what may be lost in the car market might be picked up in the grocery aisle or on the pharmacy shelf. Gradually, this view changed and, although it in some ways involves flexibilization – in theory making it possible to quickly regroup and invest more in the profit-generating industries and rein in on those yielding less profit – it was nevertheless a completely opposite trend compared to the current one. At that time, as much expertise as possible was to be gathered inside the company, so it would always be available when needed. It was also seen as a competitive advantage to have the experts on staff, so that they could not spread their wisdom to the competition. Even slack (a surplus) in human and other resources was considered important, to be able to handle things like the rise and fall in demand.[40] The dominating logic today is not the same. Organizations must be as slimmed-down as possible and external experts must be available to be called in at times when internal capacity is not enough, in terms of both expertise and manpower.

This has led to a specialization of expertise and a concentration of expertise to special competence centres, to which everyone can turn to get 'true' expertise in a certain area, rather than every organization having laymen on staff 'bluffing their way through' specialist functions. Examples of such centres include SAMC (Swedish Association for Management Consultants),

SIQ (Swedish Institute for Quality), EFQM (European Foundation for Quality Management), Adizes Institute, IHRIM (International Association for Human Resource Information Management), etc.

Conclusion

The purpose of this chapter was to show that the products and actors in the institutional environment do not exist in an intellectual vacuum. This applies in particular to products that attain widespread diffusion. One reason that they attain such widespread distribution is that they are linked to ideas, knowledge and ideologies that, during a particular time period, are expressed by many actors in many contexts. They also find support in institutional movements. Such movements, however, should not be confused with movements where people take to the streets in a collective march, or form human barricades. Rather, it is a question of indirect movements where people align themselves with a particular thinking through encountering many institutional environment products with similar content wherever they are in the world, and by encountering many actors in the environment who offer services of a similar nature.

A movement can thus be said to have arisen when the same ideas are espoused by many actors at more or less the same time in many places around the world. Once these movements have emerged, they become significant for what is perceived to be relevant and reasonable in many organizations. To not go with the flow, to swim against the current and advocate ideas other than those that almost everyone else is accepting, can be difficult, or at least create problems for the organization or individual when it comes to being seen as legitimate and credible in various contexts.

This chapter has called attention to some of the most important institutional movements in the institutional environment of organizations: marketization, organization, corporatization, managementization, and expertization. All of these movements are linked and help to fuel one another, and thus constitute a systematic force in the institutional environment of organizations, influencing what organizations want, and what they can – and do – do.

5. Societal trends

Introduction

In this chapter, we take one step further out from the individual organization. I will argue that the institutional environment does not end at movements. Instead, I will show how even these are embedded in larger contexts, contexts that span time and space – that is, that cannot be attributed to a particular place or particular actors, or to a specific time when many people happen to do and say pretty much the same thing. I call these indirect elements in the environment 'societal trends'. This should not be confused with how the concept of 'trend' is often used in everyday contexts, as a synonym for 'fashion'. By 'trend' I do not mean that which in everyday language is called 'trendy'. The concept of societal trend describes instead something that is long-lasting and deeply socialized in society.[41] According to this definition, few things can be seen as true trends in the field of organization. The discussion in this chapter therefore concentrates primarily on the content of the societal trend that has dominated general Western thinking for the past 300 years, namely, modernity. More recent streams, such as post-modernity and post-bureaucracy, are therefore only briefly touched upon here since they cannot compare with the impact modernity has had in the formation of institutional environment products and directions of institutional movements.

Modernity: the cradle of institutional movements

A first question that must be asked is how societal trends can influence organizational development. A follow-up question is whether it is necessary that the analysis stretches this far from individual organizations. And if it is, where can we draw the line for what governs how organizations develop? A first answer to these questions is that, in practice, it is problematic to attempt to specify boundaries for where an organization ends and where its surrounding environment begins, because built into the concept of the institutional environment is that it deals with something that lies outside the organization, something beyond the organization's control, that the organization must adapt to. It also means that there is always something outside the individual context that has importance for the development that occurs within. This means that there is something beyond management's reach – that market forces do not cover everything, and nor do direct institutional environment elements such as actors, products or processes. Expanding the analysis to include indirect elements such as movements is not sufficient either, because even movements have a context: they do not arise out of nowhere. There are thus factors that govern the content of movements and it is these factors that are regarded here as being covered in the concept of societal trends.

The lines between these different elements in the environment are naturally fluid in practice, and not something that the managers of organizations and other employees actively spend their days thinking about. The limits are more analytical. In practice, it is the managers, employees and other stakeholders who more or less subconsciously take the co-variation of different institutional environment elements as given. The elements are generally perceived as something that exists, and that actors and organizations must adapt to or possibly engage in to influence their form. It is also common that they are not given any particular consideration and actors simply do what they feel like, and the adaptation is therefore subconscious.

Is it important then to understand what it is that organizations adapt to, even if they often do it subconsciously? There is no absolute answer to this, but the starting point here is that this is a key understanding needed when making a serious attempt to understand how organizations work. If we do not understand the starting points for what drives us to do things in certain ways, it is difficult subsequently to change anything, or to maintain a healthy attitude toward all of the products, actors and movements in the institutional environment. Research on attempts to change organizations have shown that it is easy to change the way we talk about how organizations work – that is, how organizations are presented – but that our practice tends to be stable or that any changes actually made tend to be different than what was initially intended.[42] Such processes of decoupling and translation are discussed in Chapter 6, which focuses on how elements in the institutional environment are transformed into practice in individual organizations.

How, then, are societal trends important for the development of individual organizations? The concept of societal trends stands for something that is more stable than a fashion or a movement – it is, rather, something that is long-lasting. Both movements and fashions are more fleeting in character, fashion being the most fleeting while movements usually span longer periods of time and are encompassed by more stable organization. A trend, on the other hand, is more fundamental to our social order. The concept of societal trends thus refers to a sort of social ideal that lies beneath different manifestations that are materialized in the form of movements or more fleeting fashions. In this sense, a trend can be described as something institutionalized deep in the very foundations of a culture.

When it comes to Western culture, modernity is the most fundamental of all societal trends, though in recent decades other organization-related trends have also begun to exist side by side with modernity. Here I am thinking of post-modernity and post-bureaucracy. Both of these trends can be said to be a backlash against the premise that modernistic explanations are plausible explanatory models for why things happen the way they do. Post-modernism questions modernity's belief in the general, the rational and the objective, and stresses instead the singularity of individual contexts. Post-bureaucracy questions the individual and the isolated, and stresses the embedding of individual contexts in larger systems and contexts. Post-modernism and post-bureaucracy can be used as broad labels to describe where today's organizational research stands, research that is built on an extensive empirical basis of how organizations work and is therefore better substantiated than more idealized ways of thinking that take their points of departure in modernism. Modernism is, however, the societal trend that dominates the institutional environment that organizations operate in. Despite criticism from many directions, modernism maintains a strong, often intrinsic foothold, particularly in modern Western culture. It thereby markedly affects how we believe things work, or believe they should work.

Modernity

Modernity should be seen as an overall expression of everything we consider modern, namely the societal trend that has dominated the Western world since the age of Enlightenment in the 1700s.[43] This trend may be labelled differently in different contexts, but in the new institutional organizational analysis the term 'modernity' is generally used.[44] What it implies is that anything that occurs is considered to be a result of planned actions, that in everything that happens there is a rationality where an effect always has an isolatable cause. It is therefore also assumed that we can predict future actions. When it comes to our understanding of what organizations are and how they work and how they can be controlled, modernity is tangible. It is, however, mainly in the last century that the implications of this for organizations have been defined. Machines are sometimes used as a metaphor for this thinking and the origins of this approach date back to the early 1900s and were above all expressed in US engineer Frédéric Taylor's book, *Scientific Management*.[45] Even if the ideas have been reformulated, this machine thinking still dominates our general perceptions of what organizations are, how they work, and how they can be governed. Organization is in general still seen as an instrument that business managements have at their disposal.

Many have discussed the characteristic features of modernity, but I will not address how the concept emerged or its definitive meaning here, but will refer instead to a number of important works that articulate the views that the new institutional organizational analysis revolves around, namely the definition given by philosopher Georg von Wright and that of George Ritzer in *The McDonaldization of Society*, as well as sociologist John Meyer's definition of the concept in several scholarly articles.[46] My discussion will be based on the features of modernity collectively put forward by the noted authors, namely progress, development, and growth.

Progress, development and growth
Von Wright discusses the overarching characteristic features of modernity and suggests that it is ultimately about our constant striving for progress and growth. He suggests that one characteristic of modernity is that it can be described as an underlying stream of why we do certain things at all.[47] Modernity expresses humans' constant desire to become better and to evolve, and of our desire for more positive progress and less traditionalism. Thus, it is assumed that there

is an accumulation of sorts here, whereby earlier progress forms the basis for what is to come, and that things always get better. Knowledge becomes better, efficiency and the use of resources improve, materials get better, techniques (both social and material) improve, etc.

That this way of thinking is deeply institutionalized in modern-day society becomes apparent when we consider the opposite – that is, that someone would strive to become worse, to stagnate, and that there should be more of what is bad! If, for example, a politician or a CEO were to express him or herself in such a way, this person would hardly attract many voters or support from owners and other stakeholders. People who are not in positions of power and are therefore not dependent on being seen as legitimate in the social circle in which they operate, or by the public who chose them as their representatives, need not follow modernity's ideal. It makes it difficult, however, for them to act on a broad front; rather, there may be sporadic, local attempts to build activities or a social life. To speak in terms of counter-movements is therefore not accurate. A current example of an attempt at a counter-movement is what is sometimes called the 'slow movement' (though it does not live up to the meaning of 'movement' as defined here). Post-modernism as a whole, under which the slow movement can be classified, is also an example; but when it comes to the impact on the shaping of society and organizations in general, such elements have as yet been extremely marginal.

In organization theory, it has even been claimed that such thoughts are immoral.[48] The whole point of organizations is that organizing should be a more efficient way of coordinating resources than via markets. In that hierarchies exist, with clear chains of command, we avoid constant negotiations about the value of different goods or services in the refining processes. Organization should thus be a more efficient form of coordination than the market in some cases – that is, where the transaction costs are lower.[49] That is, if the cost of producing a good or service is lower when the organization form is used rather than the market form, then organization should be chosen. The reverse is naturally assumed to be the appropriate choice when the conditions are reversed.

All ideas and models that build on the construct of growth, development and progress have the potential to be regarded as legitimate, but this does not mean that they are also correct descriptions of how things work. They are, however, consistent with the expectations people generally have for organizational processes. Thus, we are dealing with beliefs that are deeply institutionalized in modern society. We associate the idea of growth, progress and development with modernization – that everything becomes more modern.

The concept of 'modern' in this context thus means the opposite of 'old-fashioned', but this should not be confused with what we mean by something that is 'in fashion' or has gone 'out of fashion'. It is a matter of something having evolved further, having become better, more efficient, more calculable, predictable and controllable. I will illustrate this with some examples from everyday life. If we think, for instance, about how we communicate with each other, the assumption is that texting is better than Morse code, talking on the phone is more efficient than meeting in person, and teaching is better and more efficient if we use a video projector rather than overheads or writing in chalk on the blackboard, etc. If we think about how we use technology, the assumption is that using a computer is better than typing on a typewriter or writing by hand, that driving a car is better than taking a horse and cart, that electricity is a better way of producing heat and light than using wood stoves or oil lamps. We also believe it is better, more efficient and healthier to store food in electric freezers and refrigerators rather than in an icebox cooled with ice collected from a lake in winter and stored for the rest of the year under an insulating layer of sawdust and hay.

But is it really that simple? From an efficiency standpoint, it is obviously better that we are able to heat our houses in the winter, but is it progress that we at the same time acquire problems with allergies and mould? The same question can be asked about the efficiency of travel. The fact that we can be transported quickly over vast distances by car, plane or rocket creates many possibilities, but with this comes the problem of environmental pollution due to the burning of fossil fuels, which produce high levels of carbon dioxide. The ability to do a lot in a short time also creates stress. Neither pollution nor stress evokes associations with progress. We also see paradoxical relationships in the workplace revolution that using computers for various work tasks has given us. There is no denying that it has increased the efficiency of work performance, but this brings with it problems of burn-out and unemployment, and a rapidly growing consumption of electrical energy. In the area of entertainment, we have moreover seen a development whereby we can, at any time of the day or night, entertain ourselves in our homes by watching TV, playing video or computer games, and listening to music; or buy pre-packaged, ready-to-eat food to heat in our microwave ovens. At the same time, obesity and problems with bodily functions have become a concern, since all living beings were made to move, to be in motion. We are, in addition, social beings, who want to spend time together and do things in a group. For many, meeting people and talking in person may therefore be a greater source of pleasure than sending a text or an email. From a purely technical standpoint, some progress may be better and lead to undeniable gains in efficiency. Nuclear power, for example, may be the most efficient method of producing energy we know of. Yet there are many who oppose it because they don't think it is a sustainable way to produce energy.

Development is thus not only associated with progress on every level. Progress in one area often occurs at the cost of another. Technological progress can, for example, lead to social problems. That growth should be an end in itself is not a given either, even though it may be understood as such in modernistic thinking. We may perceive it as self-evident, but where does it say that, in the long term, societal development should be built on the notion of continuous growth? Can everything grow in all situations, and is it a given that everything that generates growth is always good?

If we turn our discussion to progress and development in the area of organization, organizational development for example is seen as something legitimate to engage in. But what does it mean? That organizations should abandon the organizational form they have, the one that led them to their current position, to resemble instead organizational forms that other organizations are said to have and to whose success they are said to be the key? That organizations must do as others do is not incontestable, but there are high expectations in society that good examples should be followed. Good examples, then, mean organizations that have achieved exceptional success. Success is then measured, as a rule, in financial surpluses, size, market share, return on capital, market value, etc. It is generally considered rational to imitate examples that demonstrate success according to these criteria, since there is then the hope that one's own organization will make similar progress and grow.

Linked to this logic is the idea that significant progress is associated with the development of machines that can produce much more efficiently what people were earlier forced to make by hand; or that, through science, we can produce pharmaceuticals and treatment methods that cure diseases better. These measures of progress are also what people generally associate with the concept. It is more difficult to measure progress objectively, for example, in research on how organizations function or are governed, how marketing is carried out, how people are affected by their work situation, or whether a certain way of reporting financial transactions is better than others.

But, regardless, thinking in terms of development, progress and growth is something modern man does more or less automatically. This is how strongly institutionalized modernity is. Below, I go into more detail about some more specific features of modernity, characteristics that together are assumed to build systems of progress, development and growth. In this context, the topics discussed will be: rationality, calculability, predictability, and instrumentality.

Rationality

Rationality is an often-used concept in institutional organizational analysis for defining what 'modernity' stands for. John Meyer suggests that it is an expression for modern man's attempt to ensure that all actions that occur can be isolated and attributed to the factors that caused them.[50] The implication is that there are strong beliefs in society that everything that occurs has, or should have, an isolatable cause. That is, there is a marked tendency for modern man to think, in most situations, in terms of cause and effect – both in our search for explanations to why things are the way they are, and, when we think ahead, about what we can do to reach a certain point we think we want to reach. The ideal is for us to follow chains of events back from something that has happened to what caused it, and forward from a plan to future actions and results. If we are able to do this, it is thought that it will lead to progress and growth, above all for individual organizations and persons, but ultimately it is about presuming that successful organizations generate more general progress and thereby growth in society as a whole. By thinking about organizational and societal development in this way, the belief is that existence becomes transparent. The assumption is thus that a rational approach enables us to predict societal development, making it possible to demand accountability, calculate it, and shape order because we know who should do what. Rational thinking thus becomes very instrumental – that is, the use of certain instruments is assumed to lead to the realization of predetermined goals.

One consequence of this mindset is that it often stresses the formal. For example, organizations are often described by way of an organization chart, where names are placed in boxes showing who decides what and who is responsible for what. The assumption is that the formal structures are in turn assumed to represent actual events. A lot of energy in modern organizations is spent creating clear, formal structures, to clarify who is responsible for what, and who should do what. In this way, order is created. We say that we do things in a certain way, and assume that what we say indeed matches what we actually do. Ritzer uses the example of how McDonald's organizes work to illustrate what this means.[51] Every employee in an organization should have clearly-defined areas of responsibility and work tasks. Assembly-line logic is a typical example of this. Even McDonald's works according to these principles. Some workers grill the burgers; others cut the tomatoes, lettuce and onions. Another group assembles everything on the bun and packages it, and yet another group works at the counter, taking the money and serving the customers, etc. Everyone does his/her piece of the work. Formally speaking, this creates order. It is easy to demand clear responsibility for different work tasks. It is also easy to control and evaluate the results of different processes and the input of individual employees.

McDonald's may be an extreme example of the coordination of social processes, but the point Ritzer is trying to make is that we observe similar tendencies toward modernization in many social areas. The traditional division of labour at a hospital, for example, is fairly consistent with the McDonald's example. The medical receptionist greets the patient, processes the payment, and shows him or her to the waiting room. An orderly then shows the patient into the examining room. A doctor carries out an examination and then sends the patient to a room where samples are taken, and it is a nurse who takes the samples. The patient then waits in the waiting room again while the doctor analyses the results. If special care is deemed necessary, the patient is then sent to a specialist. If it is the joints or other skeletal parts that are the problem, the patient is sent to the orthopedics department; if the problem relates to vision, hearing or a sore throat, he or she is sent to ENT; if it is a brain-related problem, it is the neurologist the patient sees; and so on. The same procedures of the waiting and examination rooms tend to apply again in the other wards or departments.

In recent years, however, bureaucracy of this kind has been criticized for not being efficient enough. The work still has to be divided, but fewer people should do more tasks, except at McDonald's. Banks, for example, have gone quite far in making changes in this direction. It used to be common for some people to do nothing but sit at the counter and help customers with their bills, deposits and withdrawals, and the like. Others handled accounts and savings, and still others looked after credit and lending matters. Today, it is more common for everyone to be prepared to do everything. And this also includes tasks previously seen as a porter's or caretaker's work, such as opening the mail, ordering office supplies, changing lightbulbs, etc. However, we must also keep in mind that many teller services have disappeared in that bank customers can now manage many of the tasks themselves via the internet. The argument is that this is a more rational and efficient way of doing things, and the machine has replaced human work.

What I want to show, here, is that a tremendous amount of energy is aimed at modernizing society so that things that occur can be understood as the result of a sequential course of action. We see this even in the aid we give to other countries. Much of the development assistance given by Western countries to the East and developing countries is of this nature – that is, we give them aid so that they will have the resources to develop more rational processes. The aid is given both in the form of grants and as expertise. As a rule, we use ourselves as a model – how we, in our countries, handle a particular type of problem or a particular type of issue is what we pass on to them. The logic is that we have made social progress and if they copy us they too will make progress.

Another example of rationality is the strong belief that education leads to work, and that specialized training in a field, for example, for a carpenter, electrician, doctor, engineer, auditor, etc., leads to a lifelong career in that field. We like to set goals and draw up plans showing how we are going to get there. To be taken seriously, for example, an organization must set goals that it says it wants to achieve, and draw up plans and strategies for how to meet those goals. It is then not uncommon for managers of organizations to be evaluated based on this way of thinking. After all, we can then easily check whether the goals have been met, whether plans have been followed, etc. Managers naturally have a formal responsibility for the performance of individual organizations. They are therefore often held accountable for the results of what are regarded as *their* departments. If the results are deemed less than satisfactory – that is, if they do not meet modernist-based norms for what characterizes successful business – the risk is considerable that the manager, and perhaps the entire management team, will be dismissed.

Calculability

An important component of modernity is the notion that everything can be measured and calculated. The establishment of formal structures is key, because the goal is to create units and delimit processes that can be measured. Measurability and control are therefore key components. Hence, thinking in terms of quantity rather than quality is common. After all, it is easier to measure how many pictures there are in a gallery than how good or how beautiful they are. It is also easier to measure how many students graduate from a university than how much they have learned – that is, to gauge the quality of the knowledge acquired. It is likewise easier to measure how high a salary graduates of different MBA programs from different schools make, and then compare them to the salaries of those who attended similar programs at other schools, than it is to measure how high the quality of the teaching is. The people with the highest average salaries must then come from the best program!

According to the same logic, measuring the number of written works the members of a research institute have published is becoming more established than, for example, assessing how innovative the research is. Conducting measurements of this kind is much easier than comparing the quality of the knowledge being conveyed, the teachers' input, the value of the research, etc. It is also easier to verify whether an organization has a quality assurance program and possesses certification for this than to measure the quality the organization actually has. And it is likewise easy to verify how many customers an organization has, or to judge the success of operations by auditing the accounts. The idea is that once different phenomena have been given a measure we should be able to calculate things such as the relationship between time and money spent. For example, in the 1990s, it was popular to discuss the necessity of shortening lead times – that is, the faster the performance, the lower the production costs.

Developing different measures also increases our ability to evaluate and compare different phenomena and processes. That is, we also create comparability. A clear development in this direction was seen from the 1990s onward. The OECD stresses, for example, the importance of member states using the same measuring techniques to assess and compare the results of public sector organizations. In this way, the member states become comparable and the managements of similar operations in different countries can be compared based on what is deemed to be most effective. In addition to this, rankings have also emerged, where things such as different higher education programmes and business schools around the world are compared and ranked. The *Financial Times* business magazine is an important actor in defining the measures to be compared and publishing the results of studies. Special rating institutes such as Standard & Poor's have also increased in importance, where credit ratings for large companies and nations are assigned, etc.

Predictability
The thinking is that if different activities can be measured and the results calculated, predictability will increase. Developing processes for which the results can be predicted therefore becomes important. Our predilection for setting goals, strategies to meet them, budgeting, etc., is a clear manifestation of this thinking. In most contexts, we go to great lengths to

establish predictability. Common elements in performance reviews and development reviews are managers' discussions with individual employees about how their work efforts relate to the organization's overall goal, and how the overall goal can be divided up into subgoals for the individual. The label 'management by objectives' has been used to denote this phenomenon, the whole point of which is that *laissez-faire* attitudes are perceived as problematic, since they do not facilitate evaluation of outcomes in relation to expressed intentions. That is, there is no way of telling whether what happened was planned or not, or how operations are really going. We can always check whether there is money to pay the bills, but whether the results were reasonable or why things turned out the way they did is trickier to follow up. When there are expressed goals, we can always compare the outcome to the goals. We can then evaluate whether we followed the plan or whether things turned out better or worse than expected. Expressed goals and strategies to attain them, as well as continuous evaluation of their development, enable us to measure predictability against performance on an ongoing basis. Are things happening as desired? If not, where are the deviations and what corrections must be made so that the goals can be met – that is, so that what was predicted can be realized?

Instrumentality

Setting goals is one aspect of things, but it is also a question of specifying the means by which to attain them. The whole point is to realize the goals, otherwise there is no predictability and the processes can hardly be described as rational. If the means are defined, they can also be evaluated, and calculability increases because there are more specified elements to measure and more specified processes to control. Predictability also increases if we are able to follow up the outcome of the specified elements in the realization of the goals. We can then make corrections as we go if we notice that certain elements are not leading us in the desired direction.

This thinking is based on the perception that the instrument that managements of organizations have to work with is just that: organization. They can divide workers into groups, they can give them clearly defined areas of responsibility and specify what each and every individual should do, they can divide up everyone's work into goals and subgoals, and they can also offer incentives, like bonuses of various kinds, to make employees more motivated to work toward the set goals.

Conclusion

The aim of this chapter was to show the fundamental ways of thinking that modern society rests on and thereby also the ways of thinking that form the basis for dominating views of the function of organizations. By 'modern society' I mean the societal form that has evolved over the past 300 years in particular, in connection with the industrialization of society and the spread of enlightenment. Modernism is characterized by a strong belief in rationality and the ability of scientific methods to establish the truth. When we think about how we should live our lives, how the society we live in should be developed, how organizations that affect us work, we tend to think in terms of progress, growth and development, rather than the other way around. We also tend to think in terms of rationality, calculability, predictability and instrumentality. This way of thinking strongly characterizes the content of the institutional movements discussed in the previous chapter (marketization, organization, corporatization, managementization and expertization). It thereby also constitutes the framework around which influential actors in the institutional environment build their activities, and upon which widely-disseminated institutional products are based.

6. From elements in the environment to organizational practice

Everything everywhere, but everywhere different.
George Marcus

Introduction

In previous chapters, I discussed how the institutional environment is made up of actors, products, movements and societal trends. In this chapter, I shift perspective from what the institutional environment is comprised of to how different elements in the institutional environment become components of individual organizations' practice. I will thereby discuss how institutional environment elements are spread to internal organizational development processes in individual organizations. This is broken down into two main types of activities that occur in parallel in individual organizations and others that operate in their surrounding environment: decontextualization and recontextualization. By this it is meant that elements in the institutional environment are not produced and spread on their own. For this to take place, two types of active actions are required. The first has to do with the release of information, for example, from its context (decontextualization), by packaging it in a form that gives it the capacity to be mobile – that is, able to be moved. The second type of action involves introducing decontextualized information in a different context (recontextualization) from where it was produced.

The chapter begins with a discussion of the phenomenon of diffusion and how we generally view what it involves. I then move on to a more sophisticated discussion about how the diffusion of information has to do with active actions performed by both the producers and recipients of information.

Diffusion through decontextualization

In an ideal world, the diffusion of ideas would be an easy matter. Ideas would represent knowledge and knowledge would represent the objective truth, and it would be easy to make such truths accessible to others by writing them down in books or articles. Then, when a book or article was distributed across the world, the knowledge would be spread. It would be easy if we were satisfied with this explanation – that is, that once 100 000 copies of a book had been sold, or in some cases perhaps millions of copies worldwide, then the book's content would also have been spread to all of its readers. We can naturally look at it this way. Physically, the book has actually spread to many places and readers. But is that the same as the content of the book – that is, the information that it claims to convey – having been disseminated? This last question has garnered increased attention since the mid-1990s in social science research on the dissemination of knowledge.[52]

Books are a clear example of one form of decontextualization of information. And of particular importance here are books that attain worldwide diffusion, since the ideas contained in a book that attains such a wide reach then have an ability to travel great distances and thereby also the ability to be disseminated to many people.

However, ideas can be decontextualized in other ways as well, such as in the form of exchanges, where ideas from different local contexts are taken up in direct negotiations by organizations more or less adapting to one another as they do business. In this way, ideas from the local contexts are communicated to each other. This means that they have an impact on what happens and how it happens in the new context.

These examples can be viewed as two extremes of how decontextualization can occur. In one case, certain actors turn their decontextualizations into public information in the form of books, while the other case is a matter of concrete negotiations in practice between actors who have business exchanges.

Thus there is not just one channel through which all information streams out. In contrast to medical science, for example, the social sciences do not have a role whereby all information must be substantiated through scientific study, and then approved by the National Board of Health and Welfare or other body such as the National Food Agency (something along the lines of an 'Agency for Management Techniques'). Instead, as discussed in previous chapters, there are a number of other actor categories involved in producing information and rules for others, and no one is responsible for certifying certain actors as credible and trustworthy disseminators of information and producers of rules.

A clear example is consultants. Many studies try to claim that consultants are carriers of information and that information thereby follows them into their client organizations.[53] Here, it can naturally be a matter of different types of information – that is, information in different areas of expertise (law, economics, leadership, auditing, investment, financing, organization, IT, etc.).[54] For example, consultants can be assigned to investigate certain working conditions in an organization and propose solutions for how conditions can be improved. Often this involves the expression of ideas. The consultant draws the organization's attention to the existence of a certain idea. If the idea seems like a good one to the members of the organization, they may try to use it to change their behaviours in various situations.

Another example of the diffusion of information is standards like ISO 9000 (quality management) and ISO 14000 (environmental management), or through codes of social responsibility (corporate social responsibility). These codes and standards often lay claim to expressing practical, relevant knowledge on how organizations that are efficient and viable in the long-term should work. Here it is a question of deliberate attempts to spread a special form of knowledge or attempts to realize ideas through dissemination – that is, by materializing them to a format (standard) that can be disseminated in the same packaging to many people. These standards are developed on a meta-level – that is, within the framework of activities run by various types of partners and interest organizations like the ISO, OECD and EFQM. When local organizations begin to notice that such a materialization exists, they also become receptive to it. The likelihood increases that a demand for it is created, and organizations will want to implement it and become certified as purveyors of it. On the surface, we can then talk about how standards (for example, of quality management such as ISO 9000) have attained wide diffusion – at least in the sense that the packaging has been distributed to many.

However, diffusion of information does not only occur as finished products in packaged form – that is, not only through the packaging and mediation of information in a text (such as a book or standard) or talk (such as direct negotiations or presentations). For example, consultants can physically carry books and standards when they travel between organizations on different assignments. In this way, they become distributors of information, but it is not uncommon that developments occur during these travels between organizations and assignments. Consultants, and other categories of people who carry information with them from one context to another, are subjected to impressions and resistance along the way. It is not uncommon that this has an impact on how the content they carry with them is presented when they arrive at the next organization.

A number of studies on how diffusion occurs in practice have indicated that the carriers of information are only cogs in a chain of translation.[55] This means that, in practice, different mixes and combinations of different information, models, standards, etc., occur. What a consultant delivers in one context, for example, can therefore differ from what is delivered in another context, depending on what may have happened along the way from when the consultant delivered a service for one organization to when the service was delivered for another, although the same packaging of information was used in both cases. Thus, the service in question may entail the same standard, yet the delivery may differ, and hence also the results of the delivered service in the client organization. Consultants often translate the content of standards into advice or concrete models that they propose as solutions to problems the organization perceives it has, or that a consultant has pointed out that the organization has. This means that even if concrete products in the environment, in the form of books or standards, constitute the packaged content of the information delivered, the content that is unpacked, or the way in which the content is delivered or presented, is not decoupled from more indirect environment elements, such as movements and societal trends.

This naturally also applies to the decontextualization phase – that is, to the processes where information is taken from one or more contexts and pieced together into explanations that are assumed to apply to other places as well, for example explanations packaged in a book. Thus, the decontextualization phase is itself not context-free: even this occurs in contexts that have an impact on the author of a book, for example, with respect to what his or her attention is focused on and what explanations, examples and references the arguments are built around. The author then translates his or her interpretations into text, normally in the hope that a particular readership will find the text particularly relevant.

Ideas that become popular in a productized format don't just suddenly fall from the sky. And neither can we be certain that they are correct representations of what is reported to have happened in a certain context. We can say, beyond a doubt, that it is a matter of decontextualization; but there is always some uncertainty about what content is being decontextualized. This applies especially to ideas that attain wide diffusion and are in fashion for a certain period of time. Studies of what popular management ideas represent have indicated that they tend to be strongly anchored in dominating movements like marketization and societal trends like modernity.[56] Even though examples from specific organizations do exist, it is still clear that general ideas colour the content. One could say that local conditions in specific organizations in these contexts tend to be clad in language and thinking that is strongly linked to the movements and societal trends that dominate in the surrounding environment, and in the formats and specific ideas in fashion on the particular occasion and in the context in question.

When the same ideas exist in many places at the same time, it is not unusual that we perceive these ideas as very important and relevant. It has to do with the logic of following fashion. We want to do what others do, and especially those who for various reasons hold high status and represent success in the social circles we live and work in, or want to belong to. Since the 1990s, for example, there has been no systematic questioning of the ideas about the distribution of resources that dominate the management and organization discourse, namely that market transactions are the best way to realize modern ideals, like rationality, progress and growth.[57] In various different contexts, we are instead reminded time and time again of dominating ways of thinking, as they are materialized in books, standards, codes, advice, etc. In this way, these modes of thinking gain the power to both take hold and expand to areas where they did not fully bloom earlier.

Management culture has spread, for example, from the private to the public sector, and also from North America out across the Western world, and on into the former Eastern Bloc, the Middle East, Asia and Africa. This has happened in part by students from these countries attending business schools in the US and other parts of the Western world, and then moving back home and working with their newly acquired knowledge there, and in part through multinational companies establishing themselves in new countries. But it has also occurred through internationalization of the consulting sector, where certain firms with a North American base have established offices in many countries around the world.[58] Business schools and universities also establish satellite units in other countries, or offer distance education in various forms. Bringing in teachers from the US is not uncommon either. Certain books, even those of US origin, have also spread worldwide, and this has understandably had significance for the kind of ideas that people around the world discuss. In addition to this, even activities undertaken by various different partner and interest organizations that promote world peace (UN), world trade (WTO), the protection of human rights (ILO, Human Rights Watch), and the betterment of the global environment (Greenpeace) have played a part here.

Thus, ideas are spread through the types of channels just mentioned – from organization to organization, culture to culture, sector to sector, and individual to individual. And consultants who move between many organizations are affected by all of this in their travels; as are their clients. They are not insulated from impressions from movements, societal trends or fashions either. We are all made aware of what is assumed to occur in other contexts. Depending on how important we perceive this to be for our local situations, we allow ourselves to be influenced by the ideas in various ways.

What I have been trying to show here is that institutional environment elements are not neutral or objective. That is, they do not 'exist' for us as individuals and organization members unless we make them into subjects – that is, we become aware of them and recognize their existence. A prerequisite for being able to recognize the existence of something outside of what is happening in the moment right before our eyes is that ideas be decontextualized. Decontextualization is what enables information to be diffused between situations, organizations, societies and cultures. Materialized decontextualizations of local representations and general fashions, movements and societal trends give things that we are unable to see with the naked eye or experience with our own bodies in a specific context the capacity to become tangible in new contexts.

It is important to note here, however, that even when there are no direct environment elements, such as a specific book, model, piece of advice, etc., we may still be affected by indirect elements in the environment. Direct environment products that become popular go hand in hand with indirect elements such as movements and trends. They are expressions of them. This means that movements and trends are fundamental and exist in local contexts even if they are not materialized in text or talk. We can therefore be fooled into believing that they are less important because they don't have the same manifest materialization as something like a book, a standard, or the advice of a consultant.

Decontextualization – of what?

What is it, then, that is decontextualized and packaged in formats that enable physical distribution to many places around the globe? We touched briefly on this question above in connection with my claim that it is not uncommon that ideas that become popular tend to go hand in hand with institutional movements and trends. However, let me back up a bit and reconnect to modern society's ideal regarding the diffusion of ideas in society. The modernistic ideal is that decontextualization should be scientifically grounded. The thought is that science develops knowledge that is then disseminated and ultimately consumed. But what, then, is knowledge?

What people associate with science is above all the natural sciences, where researchers develop knowledge, for example, about how diseases originate and how they can be cured. Once research has come up with a solution, then a surgical technique, a treatment method or a drug, for example, can be disseminated for use in medical care all around the world. Suddenly smallpox is eradicated or the mystery of cancer solved. We gain methods to combat high blood pressure or delay the effects of dementia. We can transplant organs and perform operations on the heart or brain. We are also quick to associate science with physics and biology, where we develop methods to extract energy, send ourselves into space, calculate the strength of different materials and constructions, or understand the genesis of life, the impact of plants on the environment, or how we can use genes to engineer better crops and counteract biological defects.

This 'progress' outlook on knowledge is an ideal that modern humans want to believe in. In medicine, it is also possible to show a connection between a patient's recovery and the treatments he or she has undergone. That is, there is usually a clear link between the medical care practised and the questions researchers are working on. Researchers and practising physicians thus work with the same questions, although from different ends. One tries to come up with solutions to known or at times even unknown problems, while the other applies the solution. There are, however, many steps involved between the production of knowledge and the establishment of treatment methods, and it is not quite as simple as research coming up with unambiguous knowledge that can then immediately be applied in practice. A solution must pass a number of instances along the way to established practice, and it is not uncommon for various knowledge claims to be pitted against each other. Therefore, it may not be the truest knowledge that moves on to the next instance; it may instead be a question of the knowledge that 'wins' out in different negotiations.[59] Similar circumstances naturally apply in the production of knowledge on physical and biological matters, in connection with it being converted into practical methods to manage processes such as energy extraction, product manufacturing and food production.

If it is problematic to say with certainty that scientific progress, the best and truest scientifically-produced knowledge, is what is transformed into practice in medicine, physics and biology, what, then, can be said about the social sciences? What kinds of ideas attain wide diffusion and wherein lie the mechanisms? Is it science or is it something else? This question is raised every year in connection with the awarding of the Nobel Prize, where prominent researchers in the natural sciences readily comment in the media about how the economic prize (Riksbank Prize in Economic Sciences in Memory of Alfred Nobel) should be withdrawn because economics cannot be considered a real science. That is, there are some who believe that a social science, in Nobel Prize discussions represented by economics, should not be considered a science. According to this view, the knowledge generated by social science researchers represents more general opinion than knowledge. Indeed, these questions have been discussed a lot over the years and I will not go into an advanced philosophical discussion of science here, but it is important to raise the question of what knowledge is in the social sciences, and what it is that is de- and re-contextualized in different contexts.[60]

The same circumstances do not exist in the social sciences as in the natural sciences, with respect to the link between scientific results and general practice in the form of development of technique, the manufacture of products, etc. Generally speaking, the role of the researcher is therefore harder to understand. There is a general understanding that teaching is needed at the university and post-secondary level, and that it is appropriate that this be scientifically based. The fact that researchers take part in the teaching is therefore not particularly controversial. Opinions vary, however, regarding what it is that is produced in this scientific research. How is it useful in practice? In physics, medicine and biology, judgements are readily made about the obvious direct links between research findings and manufacturing procedures and product development. What, then, characterizes the type of information that attains wide physical diffusion and becomes popular in the area of management and organization?

This question has been discussed from different points of departure. One is that it is a matter of simplifications and popularizations of research, and adapting it to practically relevant contexts.[61] An entire genre in social science research is devoted to precisely this – research that is called *applied research* or action research. The second point of departure is strongly critical of action research, and argues that there is a risk that action researchers adjust their findings to what the client wants to hear and thereby produce worse and less tenable knowledge.[62] I am not siding with either faction here, but refer instead to another starting point, namely that popular books should be seen as an expression of a need in society. That is, a certain type of information has become popular for a reason and it is interesting and important to try to understand what this reason is.

This particular problem is discussed in a study of the production of management books that become popular. That study shows that commercial forces clearly steer the production of information.[63] There is a clear pattern in that those who write books that they want to reach a large audience combine their writing with a commercial interest. They want to make money on book sales, lectures and consulting that builds on the topics presented in the books. One requirement for being able to run such activities is that they be commercially oriented. That is, development and dissemination of knowledge are not the main driving force; it is financial gain. This goes against the modern ideal of knowledge development and dissemination, where an interest in knowledge is assumed to be what drives it – that is, an interest in progress and producing more and better knowledge about things. The production of commercially viable knowledge thus tends to be adapted more to what the buyers of books etc. are willing to pay for than how well it matches current research in the field. What as many people as possible can be expected to be willing to buy is also what the distributors, such as publishing companies etc., are interested in marketing. As a rule, publishing activities are commercial, which means that a publisher must publish titles that have the capacity to sell in sufficient numbers. This shows that the producers live under commercial conditions. As far as book authorship itself goes, it is also common for this to be combined with consulting. The number of people who are able to make a living from writing management books is very small, but as a method of conceptualizing a service, and as a marketing tool, writing books can be important. In order for it to be worthwhile, to survive in the business, consultants must quite simply offer services and write books with the types of content that there is a demand for.[64]

In one way, this can be looked at as unproblematic. That is, it seems that consumers are getting what they want – something they consider to be practical, relevant and beneficial. What is it then that is considered practical and relevant? It turns out that one unmistakable risk is that it is only things that consumers already know about that are in demand. It can therefore be claimed that the same knowledge circulates and crops up in different packaging under different names. If we were convinced that there was a single set of knowledge on business management that was true and useful, there would be no reason to contemplate this any further. But if we believe that practically executed management is governed by local requirements and conditions, everything becomes more problematic. Would this mean that there is no certainty that the same knowledge is relevant and useful everywhere?

In my study of management books, I argue that the ideas in demand may be characterized more as ideology – that is, beliefs – rather than knowledge. This conclusion is founded on the fact that the way the information being conveyed was produced can be questioned. Motivations are seldom given for why the chosen frame of reference was chosen, how existing criticism of it has been handled, and how the information that underlies the conclusions was produced. This means that as recipients, of a book for example, we are not able to follow the reasoning backwards and form our own opinion of the relevance of the conclusions. We are left to believe – or not believe – what the author says. Often books sold in large numbers conclude with concrete advice for what a leader or organization should do to improve results.

The study indicates that a possible function that this type of book serves in society is to provide answers to complex conditions in day-to-day business that are perceived as problematic, rather than to provide detailed analyses to confirm that day-to-day organizational business, and thereby management's day-to-day business, is made up of a series of complex and at times contrasting and incompatible conditions. For example, a leader may at times be forced to make tough decisions about cutbacks or decide on big investments in things such as buildings and machinery, or to work out strategic plans for how the organization should act in the short and long term. This is difficult and complicated. It is impossible to predict what will happen in the future. It is therefore not easy to know what is right and which decision should be made. Detailed empirically-based research often underlines these problems, since this is what the studies show. An important capability that CEOs readily point out is that they have to take risks and at times hazard to rely more on intuition and experience than on calculations. Having high self-confidence is important. They must, after all, serve as a guide for the employees and for the stakeholder networks they operate in. Acting with self-assuredness in situations like this helps others to believe that the strategies advocated by management are indeed the right ones. If they believe this, it becomes a unifying force, meaning that the organization's members are all pulling in the same direction. This can be more important for an organization's success than everyone pulling in the *right* direction!

There is also another complication here. It may be that what management says is well in line with the prevailing fashion streams, movements and trends. Presenting the organization in these terms creates a foundation for employees and actors in the organization's environment to regard it as legitimate. An organization that can be presented in terms of both prevailing and the very latest modes of thinking has good prospects of being seen as an organization that meets its partners' and employees' expectations for success. It can thus be important for organizations to engage in decontextualization of ideology when the business operation and plans for it are presented, rather than to describe exactly how things really occurred in the particular context.

Diffusion through recontextualization

A fundamental problem discussed in the criticism of the notion that ideas can be packaged in fixed formats to later be spread in their original fixed meaning, regardless of where they travel, is that when ideas move from one context to another it is a question of them being in part *decontextualized*, and in part *recontextualized*.

That decontextualization has occurred is not the same as the content having spread. It has been packaged in a format (text or talk) that enables its physical distribution to many people. The packaging as such has thereby been given the capacity to travel in time and space, but in order for the content to also be diffused, it has to be received somewhere. It must be unpacked. The fact that a book has been written does not mean that diffusion of its content is therefore also inevitable. This happens only when someone reads the book, or when someone talks about the book's content, or when there is discussion of the issues addressed in the book, in different contexts. Thus, a book that sits unsold on a publisher's shelf does not equal diffusion of the content. The same applies if a book has been sold but not read. All it means is that the storage site of the package has moved from the publisher's warehouse to the buyer's bookshelf, not that the content has been unpacked.

Neither is it a given that the content has spread if the author or someone else holds a lecture on the book's content. The presentation may be entertaining and interesting, but it is not certain that the audience carries the content with them into their daily lives by transforming it into some form of action, such as discussing it with colleagues or using it in the development and implementation of ideas in day-to-day business or change projects. The presenter has engaged in dissemination activities, but if those listening do not in turn apply the content on, no recontextualization occurs. Even if further dissemination does occur, it is not necessarily so that the packaged content – that which the author intended with his or her formulations – is what is unpacked when someone reads the book or tells others about its content.

Decontextualization is only one step that makes it possible for others to share in the information and rules. For the diffusion of content to new situations to occur, recontextualization is also required. When this does happen, the idea becomes local again, but in a new context. This can be compared to going on a trip and having your belongings packed in a suitcase. What is in the suitcase is packaged. This makes it easy to take many different things with you to different places, but they have no meaning for what happens at your destination unless you unpack them. The content of your suitcase has moved, but as long as it remains packed and unused, it has no practical meaning in the new context. When you do unpack and use the contents of your suitcase, the things that were packed are transferred to a new context. Exactly what happens then, however, may vary. For example, if a traveller takes flippers on a trip to a seaside paradise, and dons them as he sets out to explore the city on foot or goes out to dinner, the result of the unpacking is very different than if he had gone swimming and used them. However, in both cases, unpacking has nevertheless occurred.

We can relate this thinking to the content of a book. When someone opens the book's cover and reads what is written there, a sort of unpacking occurs. It is not certain, however, that what is unpacked matches the author's intentions. It can very well be a question of local interpretations of the content. A second step then occurs, when the book's content is translated into action by the reader. To compare with the tourist and his flippers, the first step is similar to when he unpacks the flippers and the idea of using them either as walking shoes or for swimming is born. The second step is when the action itself is carried out – that is, a flippered walk through the city or a swim.

I will return to the translation of ideas into action later in the chapter. For now, it will suffice to say that for ideas to be diffused there must be actors who decontextualize and recontextualize them through active actions. A packaged content can be distributed to many contexts, but unless it is unpacked it is only the packaging that has been spread, not the content. Ideas do not spread like dandelion seeds on the wind or effervescence in the water. Diffusion requires active actions.

How does recontextualizing occur?

How does the reception of ideas occur? Do we just sit, passively receiving whatever is sent our way and allowing ourselves to be influenced, word for word, by the statements we are subjected to? If this were a widespread form of reception, there would be almost total uniformity of actions resulting from certain statements that attain wide diffusion. If we take a popular organizational model like BPR (Business Process Reengineering) as an example, it would mean that every organization that receives statements about this model would follow them word for word. Everyone would identify processes and invest in core activities in the same way. Recontextualization would then be synonymous with copying. It would be exactly the same as the original. All organizations that received such statements would behave in much the same way regardless of where in the world they were located.[65]

The research that has been done on the diffusion of organizational models in the past 30 years or so, however, clearly indicates that the actions performed as a result of certain organizational models having attained popularity do not automatically lead to this level of uniformity.[66] High popularity of a certain model need not necessarily equate with being able to characterize the recontextualization of the model that occurs in different organizations as copying. The fact that organizations recontextualize a popular organizational model does not necessarily mean that they also follow it word for word.

When it comes to recontextualization, there are a number of different variants. The fact that a model becomes popular does not even have to mean that recontextualization occurs at all. Models can be consumed without the occurrence of any recontextualization. It can be a question of rejection of a model or of the model being consumed in the form of entertainment or as a pretence for social exchange in connection with participating in seminars. A general model can be received in a local context in different ways and the consequences, with respect to resulting actions in the local context, can vary. Below, I will discuss the following variants of recontextualization:

- Copying
- Imitation
  - Improvisation
  - Translation
  - Decoupling

Copying

To copy something means to recreate something specific as exactly as possible. Copy machines, photography and portrait painting are typical examples. The notion of copying organized activities from one context to another, by means of a decontextual-izer's vehicle of expression (for example, a book), however, is a questionable one. There are too many elements of uncertainty involved for this to be possible. Firstly, it is impossible in practice to replicate exactly a specific organizational course of events in its entirety. Secondly, it is highly unlikely that everyone on the receiving end of an attempt to represent a certain organizational course of events in its entirety interprets what has occurred in the same way. This may be due to a number of things, such as the point at which they are involved or the particular circumstances at the place where reception occurs.

Attempts to copy can, however, occur in different ways. At one extreme, one may try to copy the whole, with the end result not being particularly similar. In this case, it could be described as an attempt to copy, but the result is variation. To illustrate what such a process may look like, we can use the concept of 'karaoke' as an example. Karaoke is a popular activity in the bar and entertainment industry, and it is not uncommon that those who take part in karaoke do so with great feeling, convinced that they sound like the original. In truth, however, the result is generally far from identical, and it is often a rather wanting version. Granted, the point of karaoke is not that the original be recreated in every new context, but that it should be a fun experience for those taking part and the audience. At the other extreme, following the analogy with music and entertainment, we have what is known as the 'cover', where the requirements and expertise needed to come close to succeeding in copying the original are greater, and the outcome can be perplexingly difficult to distinguish from the original, at least for most people. In this case, the purpose is to recreate as exact a copy as possible, and attempts that miss the mark are seen as failures. If we switch back to the organizational world, the idea of quality assurance is an example of this. There, benchmarking is advocated, where the processes in the organizations that are bestowed with quality awards should be copied as closely as possible by other organizations.

There are two methods that, over the first decade of this millennium, have been used to ensure that an organizational process maintains the highest quality. One is that organizations try to become certified according to an ISO standard, in quality management (ISO 9000) or environmental processes (ISO 14000), for example. The second is that organizations try to win a quality award, or at least be assessed by a quality committee. Comparisons of the two have shown that both methods start with the same basic model for organizational quality – that is, the TQM (Total Quality Management) model.[67] The different variants then value different competencies from the general TQM model differently. The point of both models, however, is that only organizations that recreate the model well enough can qualify for certification or receive a quality award. Deviations or an organization's own variations are not rewarded. Today's higher education also sports an example of this in the form of EQUIS accreditation, which is only granted to education programmes that meet clearly specified criteria. Education programmes that want to obtain this accreditation must adapt their practices such that they are able to achieve the right measures, and naturally also a sufficiently high score on these measures. The idea is thus that, in the examples given here, an ideal be copied as closely as possible.

In the example of the two extremes of copying mentioned above, karaoke and cover, the aim of the actions is different, and so are the consequences of the actions. In the case of karaoke, the main goal is to have fun, and – if you haven't had fun – you haven't succeeded. In the case of cover, the goal is to create as close a likeness as possible; otherwise you haven't succeeded. In karaoke, it doesn't matter whether similarity to the original is achieved or not, whereas this is precisely the point with cover. In both cases, however, copying is the approach itself. It is this that one attempts to do.

Imitation

The meaning of imitation referred to here is an attempt to be like something. It is thus not an attempt to copy, but rather a matter of trying to imitate the main characteristics of an original idea or of an organizational model. Even here, we can draw on illustrative examples from the entertainment industry. A separate entertainment genre has been established where artists impersonate others. They try to imitate their mannerisms, how they talk and move, the way they express themselves, and the kinds of things they usually say. In contexts such as these, it is as a rule a comedic effect that the performer is after, and characteristics are therefore exaggerated a little here and there to achieve this. When it comes to imitation of organizational models, it is more the characteristic features associated with success that organizations attempt to imitate. It is then not a matter of copying everything from the original, but only these distinctive characteristics. With imitation, the intention is often a certain freedom to create one's own variant of the original, but not to the extent that we can mistake that it is still a question of, for example, implementation of BPR.

The concept of 'imitation' is often used in organizational literature as a collective description of organizations' efforts to imitate organizational ideals or successful examples.[68] It is noted that these efforts seldom lead to the copying of generalized organizational ideals or other organizations' structures. In the effort to implement specific ideas, as a rule there generally occur instead events that make modifications of the original idea necessary. If we again use the impersonator as an example, there are always certain physical limitations that make an exact copy impossible, but the result can nevertheless be very like the original. Even in organizations, different individuals constitute limitations on what can be implemented, but there can also be structures in the form of ownership, capital, assets and social relationships, that limit the possibilities of exact implementation of specific organizational ideas.

The recontextualization forms of improvisation, translation and decoupling represent specifications of what can happen when organizations try to imitate specific organizational or management models.

Improvisation

Improvisation can be seen as a variant of imitation. The meaning of the concept is that it is not a question of mimicking the general idea, but rather of forming a starting point for actions. In improvisation, it is the general ideas that form the basis upon which actions then rest. It is then a matter of variants or different interpretations of an original, but not to the degree that one can mistake what is being improvised.[69] With improvisation, however, it is never a question of a real attempt to copy, but of making our own version, our own interpretation of an original. However, nor does improvisation have to do with inventing something completely new, but of using something well-known as a basis and developing variants or interpretations of it. What variants are conceivable and just how much they can vary from the originals depends on the context in which the improvisation is taking place. Only improvisations that fall within the framework of the structures of the context have the potential of becoming accepted. An improvisation that deviates too much will probably be rejected.

A good example of where improvisation is a well-established practice is in the world of jazz. However, the same rules do not apply for what kind of improvisation is acceptable in all types of jazz music. As in all art forms, there are also different genres within jazz. For example, there is a big difference between Dixieland and bebop, and anyone who follows the rules of one genre when performing in a context where the other is expected will experience problems of credibility. Just anything does not work just anywhere. In Dixieland music, the structures are fairly simple and the individual artist has relatively limited room to vary. Bebop, on the other hand, pushes the limits. Each context has its fundamentals – for example, a certain tempo, certain harmony shifts, certain keys, or a certain basic melody. Each individual context can also have clear structures for how a piece should begin and how it should end, though what happens in between can be fairly unrestricted. It has to be acceptable to one's audience and co-musicians, however, otherwise the result will not be appreciated. Between genres, there are often fairly well-defined boundaries. The types of improvisations that are legitimate in one context rarely fit in another. What all jazz improvisations have in common, however, is that there is a basic structure, a language, that the improvisations must use as a starting point. It is a matter of keys, harmonies, notes, nuances, rhythm and tempo. There are standards for what combinations of these are established in different genres and, if the improviser has a good knowledge and feel for them, his or her improvisation can be adapted to produce something that has the potential to gain legitimacy in the individual context.

Improvisation typically occurs in one of two situations. One is when an actor feels uncertainty about which variant of an original is called for in a local context (for example, a certain organization or audience). The other is when people – for example, members of an organization – seek inspiration from different places and work together to come up with a strategy for the future. In this case, they usually work from known models and improvise around them. A combination of the two forms is often used in consulting.[70] In the introductory phase of a business relationship, many consultants are uncertain of what the buyer of their services really wants. During the course of the project, they then happily improvise a solution that they describe as specially tailored to the client organization, in which components of various known models may be borrowed and used as a basis. The point of improvisation is that it should not be too much like the original, but nor may it deviate too much because there is then a risk that the solution will not be accepted.

Improvisation is a common element in how professionals operate, in part those who work in strictly regulated professions like medicine, law and auditing, and in part those in more diffusely delimited professions such as CEOs and consultants of different types. A doctor, for example, often has to make a rapid assessment of a situation, and quickly evaluate the impressions he or she receives and the test results generated, to then make an intervention. The doctor must have the expertise to handle the situation that arises. There is naturally more than one way to treat a certain symptom, but the doctor must choose a method quickly. Lawyers must likewise handle situations that arise. They must assess the situation and weigh alternative avenues of action. Even the auditor must be able to handle complex situations and make choices. Although different professionals in different professions must handle different types of work tasks, what they nevertheless have in common is that the situations that they have to handle are usually complex. This means that there are many variables they need to take into account and form opinions about, to then choose ways of handling the situation. Against the background of their knowledge and experience, and their trained ability to seek information and evaluate it, their work can be described as having clear elements of improvisation.

Improvisation is not something that only occurs among formal professionals, however. It is also a significant element in the recontextualization of ideas. A clear element in how consultants work is that they have a lot of knowhow about current methods and popular techniques. In their contacts with potential clients, in order to win their confidence, it is common that consultants do not lock themselves into a particular technique but instead feel their way and make decisions as they go about the kind of solution the client is interested in. Thus, they start with what they know and improvise their way through negotiations with the client. Similar processes take place with the clients. They may not always be entirely sure of what kind of service they need, and they therefore improvise their way through negotiations with the consultants. Even once a consultant has delivered his/her service, it is common for the organization to improvise around the proposed solutions delivered by the consultant. They may not follow the consultant's suggestions to the letter, but may create their own version of it.

Translation

Translation is, along with decoupling, the term most used in the institutional organizational analysis to describe attempts made in organizations to imitate successful examples or generalized models. The reference is actually to what the process of improvisation results in.[71] That is, improvisation is what people involved in processes that end in translations of general ideas do. An improvisation, however, is a one-time event that does not result in anything long-lasting. When we can talk about a translation having occurred, other processes are at work. Here, for example, what a consultant has produced through improvisation is transformed into action in a new local context. In translation, a step-by-step process occurs whereby an idea is successively changed as it moves all the way from the idea stage to new action in a particular organization. The concept of 'translation' can thereby be defined as a completed recontextualization – that is, the final form an idea takes when it is recontextualized in a new context. This differs from improvisation, where new temporary versions are created in the moment.

In translation, an original changes into something else. Either the model gets a new name, or a new version of the original is developed when the idea is transformed into action. We usually talk about the adaptation of a general idea to something that feels meaningful in a particular local context.[72] This means that even if the same general idea can be popular and widely diffused, the actions performed when the idea is recontextualized can be quite different. An example of how this can happen is the whispering game. In the whispering game, one person whispers something into the ear of another, who then whispers what they heard to the next person, and so on. If this continues down the line in a large group of people, it is likely that what the last person in the chain says will differ considerably from what the first person whispered. When we speak of translation, we thus mean that the result of a recontextualization tends to become different from the original. One explanation for this may be that the closer to practical implementation efforts get, often the harder it gets to copy someone else's behaviour. It may also be that attempts to copy don't seem very meaningful. What then remains of the original idea, in the day-do-day organizational activities, can be called translation – or, in other words, the idea has been translated into something perceived as meaningful in the local context.

In a study of the diffusion of popular recipes for management, the concept of translation is defined as something that occurs along a chain – that is, as in the case of the whispering game, there are several categories of actors involved.[73] This can be authors of books, consultants who use models expressed in books, buyers of consulting services in organizations, managers in organizations where consultants have supplied services, or employees in organizations where consultants have worked. The journey of specific 'recipes' into local organizational contexts can be traced through such chains, and it is likely that translation occurs in all of the links of the chain. But it can occur in different ways. It can be a matter of the idea being concretized in the local context – that is, of it gaining a local meaning when it is coupled to local activities. It can also be a question of partial imitation – that is, where some parts of the idea can actually be copied in practice, but where other parts have to be translated. It can also involve a combination, in the sense that elements of different ideas are linked together and combined into actions that become meaningful in the local context. Yet another form of translation is when an idea becomes melted down, such as in the whispering game where it quite simply changes form along its journey, for example, from a book to action in a specific organization. Sometimes these processes occur consciously, but it is also something that occurs unintentionally.

Decoupling

A third variant of attempts to imitate can be described as *decoupling*. The meaning of this concept is that different types of actions are taken apart, or de-coupled. Together with translation, this is the most common concept in the institutional organizational analysis used to describe what happens when organizations try to implement general ideas.[74] For example, an organization may be presented in one way, while other actions occur in another way. It can thus happen that an organization recontextualizes a popular organizational model in talk, in its presentations of its activities, but that it does not follow the model in its other actions. The reverse can certainly also be true – that the organization follows a popular model quite closely in its physical actions, but that it does not present itself in terms of that model.[75] Decoupling can thus occur in different variations. One variant is where an organization makes the decision to introduce a certain organizational model, but then avoids implementing it in practical actions such as talk or activities.[76] However, quite often it is easy to implement a model in talk – that is, through presenting the organization in terms of a quality assurance model, for example. It is also relatively easy to implement a model in decisions, even if this may require negotiations.

This means that as long as we keep to the formal level, such as decisions and presentation, we can implement almost anything, but when it comes to transforming these things into physical activities it generally becomes problematic. Implementing a model in physical activities is more complicated because it means changing what we do. Decoupling therefore often proves to be a fairly practical method for managing pressure from the surrounding environment. Saying that we do something in a certain way may satisfy certain standard-setters in the environment, at the same time as others are happy for us to continue doing things the same way as before.[77]

Conclusion

This chapter argued that the diffusion of ideas is not a magical process. Ideas do not spread on their own like dandelion seeds in the wind, but are transported through time and space by certain people lifting them out of certain contexts (decontextualizing), and making them visible to others by lifting them into new contexts (recontextualizing). It is thus a matter of actions performed by special individuals – that is, actions performed by idea producers, idea packagers, and idea recipients.

In order to understand how recontextualization occurs, and the processes through which organizations can be influenced by models, I have stressed the importance of recognizing that it can occur in different ways (copying, and imitation in the form of improvisation, translation or decoupling). It is rarely a question of either one or the other, but rather a question of various combinations of all of the variants. It is important to note that although the intention may often be to copy, what actually occurs can be decoupling, translation or improvisation. The situation is rarely reversed – for example, where an ambition to translate is expressed and the actual effect is copying.

7. The institutional environment and organizational change

Introduction

The main purpose of this book has been to specify key components of the institutional environment surrounding organizations in order to understand how the institutional environment is related to organizational change. The point of departure was the lack of cohesive discussion in the organization and management literature where this is placed in focus. This is surprising since the institutional environment is extremely important for the development of individual organizations and what decision-makers are able to decide. The arguments in the book have therefore been structured on a model where I used the first five chapters to specify what the institutional environment is made up of. In the two final chapters, the discussion shifts to how the institutional environment affects individual organizations, and thereby also decision-makers in these organizations.

In the previous chapter, I argued that elements in the institutional environment and organizations are linked through the processes of decontextualization and recontextualization of institutional products. In this chapter, I discuss why organizations do this. Why do organizations and CEOs around the world subject themselves to the difficulties of trying to live up to the demands of the institutional environment? Can organizations and their managers not just ignore this and go about their business? Is it possible for organizations to resist change or handle pressure from the institutional environment in other ways?

Institutional demands on organizations

The short answer to the question of why organizations cannot simply ignore what goes on around them is that they are not extended the legitimacy needed to run their activities if they violate the demands of the environment materialized by institutional environment actors and their products. There is then a risk that customers and suppliers will not want to be associated with them, that financiers will call in loans and hold back on investments, etc. But what, then, is an institutional demand? Earlier in the book, I explained this in terms of it being a matter of legal, social or mental demands. Regardless of the nature of the demands, they represent various indicators that specify what organizations must do and how they must do it, as well as what they may not do, to gain legitimacy. If an organization does not follow the indicators, or does not adapt well enough, it may be dismissed as not credible.

In previous chapters, the different types of elements in the institutional environment were kept separate in an aim to define their specific nature, enabling us to recognize them when we see them. In the model depicted in the first chapter of the book, we also saw the different categories of elements as sediments of the environment. In that context, the environment was described as something that is laid, layer upon layer, around an organization. The most visible, direct relationships with other actors, followed by the immediate institutional environment, were described as the layers closest to the organization. Beyond this, I argued, lies the wider institutional environment. As a reminder, the model's arguments are illustrated in Figure 7.1.

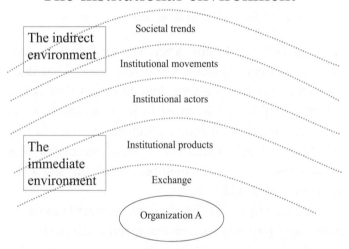

The institutional environment

The indirect environment

Societal trends

Institutional movements

Institutional actors

The immediate environment

Institutional products

Exchange

Organization A

Figure 7.1   The institutional environment's demands on organizations

The purpose of likening the relationships between an individual organization and its environment to a hill of sorts, was to paint a picture of there being collective pressure on an organization with respect to what it must and can do. The point is thus that the environment exerts various types of pressure on organizations, but that, in many cases, this pressure lacks obvious hierarchical structures. The purpose of the model was to show that the institutional environment thereby limits individual organizations' room to act.

In the remaining part of this closing chapter, I will attempt to explain why organizations feel that the institutional environment constitutes a collective source of pressure that they must somehow manage.

Not the same for all organizations

All organizations do not experience all demands from the institutional environment all the time. That does not mean that the pressure does not exist, but rather that much of it, as discussed in previous chapters, is structural and has an indirect impact by contributing to building legal, social and mental structures that organizations and their members work in and consequently must adapt to.

Some of the actions performed in organizations to adapt the business to environmental demands are carried out consciously, but many activities are also subconscious, in that organizations subconsciously follow or adapt to demands from the wider institutional environment. Still other actions are performed because we perceive tangible pressure from the immediate institutional environment regarding things that we must or are expected to do in a certain way in a certain situation. One way that the wider institutional environment manifests itself is seen in the fact that organizations perceive themselves to be in the middle of a movement where everyone else is doing things in a certain way – for example, outsourcing analyses, reception services or manufacturing. The pressure on organizations from the environment can therefore not be described as neutral or inevitable. Rather, it is more a matter of individuals and organizations more or less consciously perceiving that the pressure is there.

What characterizes the demands of the institutional environment, as opposed to demands made by actors that organizations have business exchanges with, is that here it is a question of demands that are rarely explicit and are as a rule not expressly set by a particular actor. They can instead be seen more as implicit – that is, they are built into our conscious-ness, often as something we take for granted, which we do not question.

An example of how organizations feel they must respond to demands from the institutional environ-ment can be taken from Swedish government. In a government bill from government to parliament dated 5 March 1998, the government states its intention to focus more on the quality of public operations. The proposition states that the Swedish administration shall 'be at the forefront of quality from an inter-national perspective'.[78] Furthermore, the formation of a new authority for quality development and skills provision in public administration is proposed. The proposition is based on work carried out by the administrative policy committee appointed at year-end 1995–1996, whose final report was presented in March 1997.[79] It is worth noting that nowhere in this report, or in the interim reports published within the framework of the committee work, was quality or the formation of a new quality authority (a National Quality and Competence Agency) put forward as a special strategy to be undertaken by the state. In other words, the drive for the quality initiative would appear to come from somewhere other than the reports of the committee itself.

This example suggests that organizations are not able to resist certain ideas at certain times. Why not? In the following, I will test two contrasting explanations for why we are unable to resist certain ideas: the spirit of the time, and organizing in the institutional environment.

Organized spirit of the time

In the earlier new institutional organizational analysis, our not being able to resist certain decontextualizations is depicted as being due to an almost mystical force, a magnetism that inevitably draws us in.[80] In some ways, the pressure of the institutional environment can be perceived as magical or magnetic in practice. As an explanation as to why we cannot resist certain ideas, however, it is not particularly satisfying.

Some institutional environment products become more popular than others. This need not be due to their being better or more true, but precisely, as with clothing, music, and lifestyles in general, certain ideas become fashionable. And precisely as in other areas, individuals have a tendency to be rather uncritically swept along with the waves of fashion. The fact that organizations are unable to resist certain ideas could then be explained by the fact that they simply follow the fashion. Following the fashion is manifested in our giving certain ideas about organization and management the power to guide our actions. But as an explanation, it is still extremely vague and rather mystical. Why are we unable to resist the fashions?

Let me attempt to answer this question by first stating that a fashion does not come into being on its own. The reason that new fashions are created is that certain actors perform certain actions. In the clothing industry, fashion designers invest great efforts in designing new styles that should preferably be different from last year's fashion. If this year's collection were no different from last year's, there would be no reason for consumers to buy new clothes (unless their old ones had worn out, that is). Substantial resources, then, are used by clothing distributors to market the new clothes for the season. There is also a group of actors dedicated to commenting on the season's new clothes via different types of media (especially TV and magazines). Together, these activities help to standardize the 'rules' – that is, what is *in* and what is *out*, what is fashionable at the moment. All these commentators telling us what is currently in fashion thus shapes our perceptions about clothes. If we feel that we deviate too much from the 'ruling' fashion, a demand arises in us for new clothes. This can be compared to a demand for music performed by certain artists. It is, after all, not that one person's or group's music is *better* than another's in an objective sense, but they have been marketed by their managers, record companies and concert organizers so appealingly that, for many of us, it makes their music appealing too. If the marketing is successful, it can help to create a demand for a particular group's recordings and concerts.

When it comes to popular culture in the clothing and music industries, this simple analysis seems fairly obvious. But when it comes to immaterial phenomena, such as ideas about organization and management, it can be more difficult to think that even here there is a fashion industry at work. Ideas about organization cannot simply exist on their own in the same way as clothing or music fashions. It is more a matter of the actors around an organization engaging in different ways of organizing the surrounding environment. This leads to certain actors and certain products being established as especially important. Depending on how systematic the organizing is, the result can be more or less tangible. For example, a fashion such as Michael Porter's value chain may not seem especially powerful; it deals mainly with an idea that was fashionable for a few short years (in the latter half of the 1980s). But when we start to talk about ideas that have been transformed into rules, in the form of international quality standards (ISO 9000), for example, we can say that the pressure has materialized in a more tangible form. When there are rules in the surrounding environment, it is easier to understand that we have to relate to them. Following a fashion, on the other hand, is voluntary; or is it …?

To follow or not to follow ... that is not the question!

The idea of voluntariness – freedom of choice – is a complicated one. The freedom to choose! In principle, we have the freedom to choose in all situations. Each and every one of us is free to obey the law or not. It is not permissible to break the law, but we all have the freedom to choose whether or not we do. When it comes to the law, the consequences of one's choices are calculable. We can calculate the risks. For example, it is completely possible to judge how high the risk is that you will get caught if you choose to fiddle the books, or breach the terms of a signed contract.

When it comes to the law, it is thus fairly easy to conduct a consequence analysis of one's choices. One can also actively decide whether it is worth the risk to break the law or whether it is best to follow it. When it comes to norms, fashions and more fluid ideas, it is much more difficult to make active choices. That is, it is more difficult to decide how one should relate to a norm or a fashion. We may not even really know for certain that they exist in the first place, let alone that we are following them. If we break one, however, there are usually consequences. For example, if a leader appears drunk, unkempt, is generally unpleasant or uses the organization's resources to acquire exclusive homes or perks for him/herself or for friends and relatives, it is unlikely that this person will remain in his/her position for long. However, we do not react to everyone who behaves deviantly. It is a matter of degree how institutionalized and taken-for-granted an idea, norm or fashion is in a certain context. The higher the degree of institutionalization – that is, the more we take an idea (or behaviour) for granted in a certain situation – the harder it is to actively decide whether we are going to follow or violate it, and the harder it is to judge the risks of our actions. To try to judge the degree of institutionalization of an idea, norm or fashion, however, is not easy. The concept of institutionalization is quite simply not sufficiently distinct to provide a more detailed description about how different types of immaterial elements in the environment affect organizations, or whether it is even possible to make choices that go against institutional demands.

The concept of institutionalization seldom gets further than that it is the spirit of the time that guides us; that is, the fact that we live in a time when certain ways of thinking about things dominate, and guide what we take for granted. Even if the thought of being shackled by the fabric of the spirit of the time is completely reasonable, it sidesteps the complexity that lies in the diffusion of ideas. This somewhat magical explanation – that it is the spirit of the times that guides us – is therefore not satisfying. Is it some natural being that exists on its own? The sense that prevails in practice may be that there is no choice; we are trapped by the spirit of the time, a mental iron cage from which there is no escape: there is only one choice, and that is to allow ourselves to be swept along. It is like a black hole, swallowing everything in its path. The explanation for this would be that we arrive in its path by being seduced into it by gurus who travel the world holding lectures, or by other means, like consulting and authoring written works, spreading their messages around the globe. To open the door, so to speak, to these people is like stepping into the path of a black hole. Once we have crossed the line, there is no stepping back. This may explain why we allow ourselves to be swept along, why we don't resist, but it does not explain how an idea becomes so timely in the first place.

Organizing in the institutional environment

In studies of the content of ideas that spread, it is clear that not just any ideas become popular.[81] Rather, it is ideas of a particular nature. Although a lot of ideas spread, a closer look at them indicates that the ones that attain wide diffusion, those that reach to many places around the world, those that are globalized, share clear, common denominators: first, they are firmly rooted in the societal trend of modernism; and second, they are in line with dominating institutional movements like marketization, organization, corporatization, managementization and expertization. This applies both to ideas that can be given the character of fashions, and to those that are then further institutionalized to become materialized in the form of explicit rules or standards.

In the following, I will show that it is neither a question of the diffusion of proven, superior general knowledge or of something magical, nor that the content can be equated to the laws of nature. Rather, it is a question of content that is the result of activities performed in interaction between particular actors, who may or may not be dependent on one another. Below, I exemplify this under three headings (*Discourse, Fashion* and *Standards*), where there occurs a gradual concretization of the institutional environment's pressure on individual organizations. Figure 7.2 illustrates the relationships between discourse, fashion and standards.

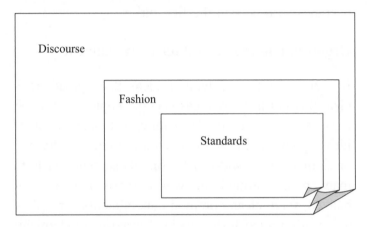

Figure 7.2   From discourse to standards

A discourse is a general conversation about something. A fashion is a specification of certain expressions in the discourse, and a standard is a mobilization of forces around a fashion. The further into Figure 7.2 we get, the more tangible the pressure of the surrounding environment; but the pressure from discourses and fashions can be at least as great, even if they have not obtained the same degree of concretization as standards that have been established in a field.

In the following, I will argue that organizing occurs at every level of Figure 7.2, but that it becomes more formally structured the further in we get. The reasoning is that it is the degree of organization that determines whether a product or actor in the environment becomes popular and gradually becomes established as a standard.

Discourse

The concept of 'discourse' can be used to denote a widely established way of talking about a certain phenomenon.[82] It is thus not an expression for a conversation between two individuals but rather a kind of public conversation – that is, a conversation made up of not only what occurs between individuals, but what can be viewed as the sum of all individual conversations about a certain phenomenon. However, a discourse comprises not only talk about a specific topic between individuals, but also texts about the same thing. That is, a discourse can be seen as a concept that summarizes what is said, in part directly between individuals, and in part in what this book calls institutional products. A discourse can be said to exist when a topic becomes established in a larger context. One prerequisite is that attention be focused on a specific phenomenon – that is, that actors of different kinds show an interest in something and begin to talk about it. A discourse can be about things like management methods or techniques, or about something claimed to be best practice. But it can also have to do with popular organizational models or management concepts, or standards for quality, environment and social responsibility.[83] The limits for what is or is not a discourse can thus be determined empirically. We can talk, for example, about the global management discourse, which refers to the total combined conversation about management that takes place in literature, teaching, consulting and practice.[84]

However, it is not a global discourse if there are no common points of reference. This means that if we were to read different books, base our teaching on different theories, and run organizations in completely different ways around the world, it would not be appropriate to see this as constituting a global discourse on management. If, on the other hand, we observe similarities in the books being read, how teaching is conducted, and how activities are organized in many places in the world, we can then say that the discourse is global – that is, that there exists a conversation with common denominators at the global level. Otherwise, it can be more appropriate to talk about different local discourses taking place, in different countries, for example. When it comes to management, it is evident, however, that there are close similarities in how we talk about management around the world. There are close similarities in the books we read and how teaching is conducted. There is also a clear and growing tendency for us to use English expressions everywhere in the world to describe things, such as occupational titles and strategies.

That general discussions about a subject become established can be seen as a first step in how the institutional environment creates pressure on organizations. But how does a discourse become established?

It is hardly possible to set an exact starting point for a public conversation, but often the diffusion of a conversation can be linked to the writing of books about a specific topic, which is later discussed amongst readers. But conversations can also start before books are written, such as a conversation between individuals in everyday life – for example, individuals in two organizations that negotiate with each other about the requirements and conditions to apply in exchanges between the organizations they represent. In this conversation, problems may be identified and solutions to them discussed. A demand for ideas may then arise, opening opportunities for actors such as consultants to pitch projects of a certain nature. Further diffusion of a discourse can occur by business journalists drawing attention to a specific topic that they write about, or by a CEO, consultant, politician or researcher writing a debate article, column or the like in a newspaper or professional magazine or journal.

To further define this, we can identify contexts of particular importance where the actors perform; that is, contexts in which conversations about organization and leadership take place. Below are some of these contexts:

- Academic education
- Seminars and courses
- Literature
- Consultancy/advisory services

Obviously conversations with different content occur within the limits of the various types of activities listed above, but conversations about a particular idea can also take place in several contexts. The lines between different discourses are often diffuse. For example, while conversations about one idea may take place in several contexts, the forms of the conversation may differ. It is common, for instance, that the way we talk about an idea in academic education and research differs from how we talk about the same idea in consultancy, popular literature and executive education courses. There may also be differences in how people talk about management in academia, among consultants, in practice, and among politicians.[85] One way of describing this is that, within the limits of a discourse, there can be various subdiscourses that drive different interpretations of the idea that the conversation revolves around.

Discourses can vary in character and this is determined by what components they are built around. Such determinants include: (1) who the actors are, and how credible what they say is; (2) what kind of data lies behind what they say; and (3) the rhetoric – that is, how the arguments are constructed.

This means that structures are established in different social contexts for what kind of talk about management is perceived as relevant. Structures are established through social interaction – that is, organizing. However, here the organizing is spontaneous – that is, no actors have been assigned to organize particular discourses. But this does not happen by itself. It requires actors – actors actively working to produce, distribute, consume, and in different ways trying to legitimize ideas and their relevance and meaning. This creates a general feeling fittingly expressed by Norwegian organization researcher Kjell-Arne Røvik:[86]

> Now, at the turn of the millennium, it is considered as almost 'right' that modern, future-oriented organizations – public or private, big or small – should work with quality assurance and quality management.

Fashion

Once a discourse has been established, clear patterns can be seen in the types of ideas the reasoning revolves around. These can be called *fashions*. It is common, however, that studies on the meaning of organizations' institutional environment take the existence of ideas, particular models and fashions for granted.[87] But there are also studies that suggest that they do not fall from the sky or crop up like mushrooms everywhere.[88] Rather, they are constructed as a result of particular activities being carried out.[89]

It has been argued, for example, that fashions are constructed in interaction between academia, management consultants and the mass media, on the one hand, and those who demand the fashions, on the other.[90] A study on the emergence of the development of US management discourse from the 1870s to the 1990s notes that, as a rule, new ideologies are initiated as a result of perceived organizational problems in practice.[91] According to the authors of the study, companies call in outside help to solve these problems. In their interpretation, the interaction between academia, consultants, the mass media and practitioners is driven by demand. This is also the explanation cited most when arguing that quality issues must play a central role in modern organizations. The suggestion is that increased competition and globalization have changed the requirements and conditions for modern organizations. Demand would then be what drives the wide range of actors that market quality models of different types.

This explanation, however, that certain organizational models attain wide diffusion and become popular based solely on the fact that there is such a high demand, does not paint the whole picture. For example, it is conceivable that one reason that those demanding quality-related services perceive their situation as problematic could be that there is a wide variety of ideas telling them that organizational forms that are not quality-assured have certain problems. If a perception grows in an organization that it has an organizational form that has been depicted as problematic, it is more or less inevitable that the organization will acquire these problems. Not because they are actually problems, but because the current fashion says such situations are problematic.[92] Organizations then become receptive to ideas that claim to solve such concerns.[93] When it comes to quality management, organizations with no special quality assurance programs may be depicted as being in serious trouble.

Thus, fashions do not simply exist. They are constructed from interaction between a number of actors. Some ideas survive the fashion phase and become further institutionalized. Others never become more than fleeting fashions. Their topicality is brief and in some respects they can be seen as conceptual experiments.[94] That does not necessarily mean that an idea disappears, but that the form in which it became popular at a certain point in time may have become 'depopularized'. The idea itself can then be recycled and repackaged in another form on another occasion or in other settings.[95] For an idea to become fashionable, however, requires a more systematic interaction between different actors than in the case of discourses. It requires that many actors do about the same thing at about the same time. Even here the element of spontaneity is tangible, however. Thus, for fashions to arise, no formal organizing – that is, where particular organizations are assigned the responsibility of creating fashion – is required.

Standards

Certain ideas do, however, survive the fashion stage to become materialized in formal, even more structured format. In order for this to occur, a systematic and more formal organizing must occur between a number of actors.[96] In this context, what it is that gives certain actor categories the authority to organize then becomes important.

Let us go back to our earlier example about quality. That a systematic and formal mobilization of power has occurred around the 'quality' fashion may explain why an agency such as the new authority for quality and expertise (National Quality and Competence Agency) was formed, and why one of the agency's first assignments was to investigate, in part, how different authorities view quality work and, in part, what the market for quality awards looks like. The investigative committee's report from summer 2000 states that:[97]

> What is important is not which of the available TQM-based methods/models an authority chooses, to work systematically with the development of their activities, only that they choose one!

This implies that systematic interaction has been established in how one thinks about organizational quality all over the world, with TQM as the basis. One effect of this is that the point of departure used for 54 national quality awards was either the European Quality Award (EQA) or the US Malcolm Baldrige National Quality Award (MBNQA).[98] Like 19 other countries, Sweden's award (the Swedish Quality Award, USK) is based on MBNQA, while EQA lies behind the corresponding national awards in 34 countries. Furthermore, at the turn of the millennium in Sweden, there were an additional 22 awards (8 regional, 3 sectoral, and 11 internal organizational) in turn based completely or in part on USK. A number of organizations also use the USK model for customer-oriented business development in their activities, even though they do not award a prize.

There is reason to believe that the same pattern exists in the other 53 countries that used either MBNQA or EQA as a basis. It can also be added that the differences between USK, MBNQA and EQA are mainly cosmetic. They all have:[99]

... the same purpose and lead to the same goals. They have a consistent form and structure ... Hence, the three models require about the same information on an organization's performance, including the financial results. The three models also place the same demands on relatability between method, application and result.

Consequently, there is reason to assume a high degree of uniformity in the content of quality awards around the world. This means that, in the area of quality, the forefront – where the Swedish government says Swedish agencies should be – is highly standardized internationally. Quality awards and quality certification, such as ISO 9000, are thus much more structured models of how quality work should be carried out than the more general quality models earlier in fashion (for example, Quality Circles, TQM and Kaizen). They are structured in the sense that organizations are established with the mandate to draw up clear criteria for what should apply for an organization to receive an award or certification. In the case of awards, this involves a point system, where organizations must attain a certain total score on a number of items that the quality award model focuses on. In the case of ISO 9000, no point system is used and it is more a matter of technical requirements regarding the documentation of procedures and charting of the organization's networks and processes, where an 'owner' is identified for each process.[100] To enable the use of the same point scale and criteria internationally, structured cooperation is required.

In both cases, it is a matter of agreements between a number of actors regarding special sets of rules that should apply for granting certification or an award. This means that there are a whole host of connections between the actors who develop and maintain the certifications and awards, and those who verify whether organizations live up to the requirements. There are thus a number of actors gathered around all of the different products and awards in the area of quality. Examples that can be mentioned include:

- Consulting firms that work with models like TQM and Kaizen;
- ISO (International Organization for Standardization), which lies behind ISO 9000, and SIS (Swedish Standards Institute), its equivalent and representative in Sweden;
- EFQM (European Foundation for Quality Management), which operates the European Quality Award;
- EOQ (European Organization for Quality), which, in cooperation with the EU, is involved in long-term work mainly with technical quality issues in society and industry;
- SIQ (Swedish Institute for Quality), which lies behind USK; and
- ASQ (American Society for Quality) and NIST (National Institute of Standards and Technology), a section of the US trade department, which operates the Malcolm Baldrige program.

But even within organizations, new actors have been constructed and old ones given new tasks. For example, many organizations have set up special organizational units exclusively to coordinate quality work in the entire organization. They hire or appoint special quality managers for different products or processes. These individuals may be assigned titles like *quality manager* or *head of quality*. The establishment of a new agency for quality and expertise in Sweden and other countries (for example, Denmark) is also an example of the emergence of new actors.

This can be described as the emergence of an organized international mobilization in quality work, where standard forms of what should be considered quality are established. A common point of reference in these efforts is the concept of 'Total Quality Management' (TQM). An important aspect of this organized mobilization of power is the cooperation between government and industry in the work on awards. In the US, a private organization, ASQ, runs the work with MBNQA together with NIST, a section of the trade department. In Sweden, SIQ, an industry research institute, runs the work with the Swedish national quality award (USK). The two principals behind SIQ, however, represent both industry and the state, via the Swedish Association for Quality (with some 100 members, mostly from industry but also from public organizations). EFQM, which operates the European award (EQA), is supported by industry but also by the European Commission. EFQM members are national quality institutes similar to SIQ in Sweden. Some cooperation also exists with EOQ, a private organization. In other words, the work with quality awards has organized support from both industry and governments.

In summary, we can conclude that the power mobilization around a particular idea about what quality is, manifested in the form of quality awards for example, began during the period 1987–1993 when a number of awards, and organizations that run them, were established in many countries. During this period, long-established organizations from government and industry also organized an aim to develop powerful instruments for national, regional (EU) and sectoral quality improvements.

In addition to this backing from government and industry, the status of the awards is further reinforced by heads of state or representatives of different nations awarding the prizes at official ceremonies. The awards thus also have a high symbolic value.

The interconnectedness of actors, which I have called an international, organized mobilization of power in an emerging sector, could thereby serve as an added explanation to the fashion theory of why organizations choose, at about the same time, to concentrate on quality strategies.

From discourse to fashion, from fashion to rule

I argued above that the following of fashion and the diffusion of ideas are not enough to explain why organizations around the world engage in special quality management initiatives today. We follow fashions because of our desire to keep up and avoid the risk of losing legitimacy. Fashions also go in waves, and what is in fashion changes. That ideas spread and some become popular and are perceived as fashions is a key explanation to why we are unable to resist a certain idea at a certain point in time. But, as argued here, ideas do not have a life of their own. If it were not for certain actors doing certain things at different stages along the way, they would not exist.

It can thus be argued that there has been, for quite some time, an extensive international mobilization of ideas, which has created a cohesive international discourse on quality in organizations. This has subsequently developed into a mobilization of power around a certain meaning of what quality is assumed to be. What has occurred can thereby be said to be that, through systematic organizing, quality has gone from being an idea to being established as a discourse, where we have seen various types of packaging, which have been in fashion for different periods from the middle of the 1980s. Since then, an international power mobilization has occurred around a specific meaning of what quality is believed to be.

Institutional demands as organized pressure

Why, then, could the Swedish government not resist focusing on quality? The example above, of the quality movement's organizing, shows that a series of events took place thanks to the actions carried out by a series of actors, independent of or as a direct result of what others did.

The quality movement example shows that institutional pressure is created through organization. In the present case, the organizing becomes more and more visible in that actors interact explicitly and this leads to the carrying out of synchronized actions. It even goes as far as the establishment of two types of international standards (ISO 9000, and international and national quality awards), which can be seen as two variations on the same theme (TQM).

Above, I have concentrated on the area of quality in an effort to provide a clear example of how pressure on organizations from the institutional environment occurs as different forms of organizing. In the case of quality, the result is pressure that is materialized in the form of international standards. Institutional pressure can, however, occur in other forms. The most obvious form is naturally legislation. Even here, it is a question of organizing in order for a law to be adopted and entered into force. But, in this case, governments play a more central role as organizers. It is, after all, only states that can make law! Laws are, in addition, binding, in comparison to standards, which are, formally speaking, voluntary to follow.

Institutional pressure can also arise in less well-defined forms, however. Cultural norms, as well as norms for a certain type of situation, organization, social network, etc., also create institutional pressure. Even these come about through actors coordinating their actions. Norms are not written down, however, and are established over time through individuals trying to find ways to interact. When certain paths of communication have been established, they are institutionalized as unwritten social codes for how we behave in different contexts. Norms can also arise through, for example, the establishment of discourses or the crystallization of fashions. When certain ideas are discussed in many contexts, and when we run into the same idea over and over again, it is not uncommon that we become accustomed to a particular way of talking and thinking about certain phenomena, such as organizational quality, or leadership, or organizational structures, etc. Out of habit, we stop questioning and take the way of thinking advocated by an idea for granted. By doing this, a norm of how we should think and feel about things in certain situations is established. In contexts such as these, however, organizing is not as formal as in the case of laws and standards. Even if no special organizations are established to set the norms in a particular field, they do not arise all by themselves. They come about through the systematic interaction of a number of actors working together over long periods of time.

When something is institutionalized ...

When something is institutionalized, it means that something whose existence we do not question has been established.[101] An idea can lose popularity – that is, it can disappear from the popular organizational discourse. But while we may stop talking about a certain model, its content may remain and continue to be discussed under another name or occur as a taken-for-granted component in decisions and actions. It has then become something generally regarded as a more or less natural part of every organization's day-to-day business. In practice, it has to do with institutional demands having been established for what organizations should be, what they should do, and how they should act – demands that organizations are not free to choose to follow or not.

This type of rule differs from laws and directives passed by some central body, because it is not binding in the sense that a formal court can impose punishments on people who break it. It is more a matter of a standard that is explicit without being formally binding. Bowing to such institutional demands, like a standard, is voluntary in the sense that no authority can demand that organizations follow them. And neither are there direct consequences for those who go against them or choose not to follow them. There can nevertheless be pressure from the environment that the organization operates in to follow the standard, since the result would otherwise be that one loses legitimacy. To illustrate the possible consequences of this for individuals or individual organizations, I refer to the following excerpt taken from the preface to Swedish business administration scholar Sune Carlson's classical book from 1951 on how executives behave, using a quote from anthropologist Margaret Mead and her study of the Arapesh people of New Guinea:[102]

> No one, it is assumed, really wants to be a leader, a 'big man'. 'Big men' have to plan, have to initiate exchanges, have to strut and swagger and talk in loud voices, have to boast of what they have done in the past and are going to do in the future. All of this the Arapesh regard as most uncongenial, difficult behaviour, the kind of behaviour in which no normal man would indulge if he could possibly avoid it. It is a role that the society forces upon a few men in certain recognized ways.

Mead studied what characterized the life people in this isolated culture lived. What Carlson is trying to show here is that there are rules, or rather institutionalized expectations, for how certain actors should behave in certain situations in society. If someone wants to play a certain role, that person must play by the rules of the game, otherwise he or she will not be accepted as a legitimate player. If someone wants to play the role of a leader, for example, the rules/expectations for what a leader does in special situations must be followed. The quote states that this is something that 'society forces upon a few men in certain recognized ways'. This is precisely what the institutional environment does: it creates legal, mental and social structures that we must work within if we want to be accepted as serious, legitimate actors. If we don't like these structures, we have three choices:

1. We can acquiesce and play the game according to the rules anyway.
2. We can be difficult and refuse to play by the rules. The risk here being great that we will not be permitted to play, that we will be regarded as non-credible and untrustworthy, someone who cannot really be counted on.
3. We can try to change the demands of the institutional environment.

To follow or not to follow … or to change

This book can be seen as a guide to all three of the above-listed strategies. By specifying key components of the institutional environment, we also specify the underlying basis that can be used to consciously choose a strategy. If we choose to acquiesce, it is good to know what it is we have chosen to accept. If we choose to be difficult, it is good to know what it is we are going against so that we do not end up as doctrinarians. If we choose the third strategy, to try to change the demands of the institutional environment, it is good to know what the environment is made up of, so that we are also able to choose where and how to concentrate our efforts.

To change the demands of the institutional environment, it is essential that we have patience and work systematically. We must operate in the circles where the demands are formulated, and acquire a position of legitimacy that enables us to be regarded as credible and to make our voices heard. We must also mobilize others to join us, so that we are not trying to move mountains on our own. This book does not provide methods for how to influence the environment. It merely draws the map and points the way, giving us something by which to navigate. Those who wish to pursue this are referred to the literature on lobbying and decision-making.

Notes

1. Meyer et al. (1993).
2. Cf. DiMaggio & Powell (1983 [1991]).
3. Scott (1995).
4. DiMaggio & Powell compiled an overview of the state of research in 1991. A more recent compilation was also done by Greenwood et al. (2008).
5. Furusten (1996; 1999).
6. Rhenman (1973); Normann (1975).
7. The 'IT bubble' is a concept used to characterize the large economic interest in IT that existed in the years around the turn of the twenty-first century. During this time, numerous consulting firms were started and vast sums of money were invested in these companies, but only a few succeeded in creating sustainable profit-generating operations.
8. See, for example, Hägg & Johanson (1982).
9. Another type of information not considered here is something we can call 'market information', which can be of a character suited more to mass audiences. An example of this is press releases, where specific information is produced, for example, to inform about new research findings in medicine. Market information is often directed to the media in the hope that it will be taken up by journalists and published in a condensed form in daily newspapers or weekly or monthly magazines, and feature in headlines, or on TV or radio news magazines.
10. Cf. Latour (1987); Furusten (1999).
11. See for example Meyer & Rowan (1977 [1991]); Djelic & Quack (2003); Djelic & Sahlin-Andersson (2006).
12. This is discussed in detail in Ahrne & Brunsson (2004) and Svedberg-Nilsson et al. (2005).
13. www.vv.se/template/page3.
14. www.ivf.se.

15. See Lindberg (2005).
16. For more on consultation as a practice and social phenomenon, see for example Furusten & Werr (2005); Furusten (2003); Kipping & Engwall (2002); Clark & Fincham (2001); Sturdy (1997); Fincham (1996); Clark (1995); Czarniawska-Joerges (1988).
17. www.skb.se.
18. The concept of 'the moment of truth' has been used by, among others, Carlzon (1985), and Normann (1982 [2001]).
19. Czarniawska-Joerges (1988).
20. Meyer (1994; 1996).
21. To read more about NPM, see for example Lane (2000); Hood (1995); Christensen & Lægreid (2001); Almqvist (2006).
22. Engelsson (2006).
23. Cf. Kubr (1996).
24. Kipping et al. (2003).
25. See for example Greiner & Metzger (1983); Gummesson (1991).
26. Furusten (2003).
27. Brunsson & Sahlin-Andersson (2000).
28. See for example Rombach (1999), and Forssell & Jansson (2000).
29. Forssell (1992).
30. Furusten, K. (2009).
31. Saint-Martin (2000).
32. This is discussed in detail in, for example, Jacobsson (1994).
33. See, for example, Forssell & Norén (2006); Lindberg & Furusten (2005).
34. Brunsson (1991).
35. Furusten & Lerdell (1998).
36. Czarniawska-Joerges (1985).
37. Rombach (1999); Brint (1994).
38. Giddens (1990).
39. Furusten & Lerdell (1998).
40. See, for example, Cyert & March (1963) and Galbraith (1973).
41. Cf. Ritzer (1993); Forssell (1992); Meyer (1994).

42. There is a lot of research on this topic, but compare for example a number of central studies such as Brunsson & Olsen (1998); Czarniawska & Sevón (1996); Røvik (2000).
43. See von Wright (1993).
44. Sometimes also referred to as the 'modern project'.
45. Morgan (1986).
46. See von Wright (1993); Ritzer (1993); Meyer (1994); Strang & Meyer (1994).
47. Von Wright (1993).
48. For example Rhenman (1973).
49. Cf. Coase (1937); Williamsson (1975).
50. John Meyer is a US sociologist who, along with colleague Richard Scott of Stanford University in California, is often referred to as one of the most influential authors in institutional organizational analysis.
51. Through his book, *The McDonaldization of Society* (1993), US sociologist George Ritzer has become one of the most cited critics of modernism in the field of organization theory.
52. See for example Latour (1987); Meyer (1994); Furusten (1996; 1999); Czarniawska & Sevón (1996); Røvik (2000).
53. See for example DiMaggio & Powell (1983 [1991]); Kipping & Engwall (2002); Sahlin-Andersson & Engwall (2002).
54. Cf. Furusten & Werr (2005).
55. Røvik (2000).
56. Furusten (1996; 1999).
57. Cf. Meyer & Rowan (1977 [1991]); Brunsson & Sahlin-Andersson (2000).
58. See for example Kipping et al. (2003).
59. Sjögren (2006).
60. To read more about knowledge in the social sciences, I recommend works such as Kuhn, (1962 [1970]); Burrell & Morgan (1979); Brunsson (1981); Whitley (1984); McCloskey (1986); Furusten (1999).
61. For example Greiner & Metzger (1983); Gummesson (1991).
62. For example Kieser (2002); Engwall et al. (2002).
63. Furusten (1996; 1999).
64. Furusten (1996; 1999).

65. See for example Meyer & Rowan (1977 [1991]).
66. See for example Meyer & Rowan (1977 [1991]); Brunsson (1989); Czarniawska & Sevón (1996); Furusten (1999; 2003); Røvik (2000); Czarniawska & Sevón (2005).
67. Cf. Furusten (2002).
68. See for example Sevón (1996); Sahlin-Andersson (1996); Sahlin-Andersson & Sevón (2003).
69. Pasmore (1998); Meyer et al. (1998); Hatch (1999).
70. Furusten (2003; 2005).
71. To read more on this, see Furusten (2003).
72. Cf. Latour (1987); Furusten (1999).
73. For a detailed discussion of this, see Røvik (2000).
74. For a detailed discussion of this, see for example Meyer & Rowan (1977 [1991]), and Brunsson & Olsen (1998).
75. To read more on this, see Fernler (1994; 1996).
76. Brunsson (1989) discusses this in detail.
77. See also Brunsson & Olsen (1998), where this is addressed in detail.
78. Proposition (1997/98:136, p. 19).
79. SOU (1997:57).
80. Cf. Meyer & Rowan (1977 [1991]) and DiMaggio & Powell (1983 [1991]).
81. See, for example, Furusten (1996; 1999); Djelic (1998); Gammelsætter (1994).
82. Foucault (1971 [1993]); McCloskey (1986).
83. Cf. Furusten (1999).
84. Ibid.
85. Furusten (1996; 1999).
86. Røvik (2000, p. 13).
87. See for example Meyer & Rowan (1977 [1991]); DiMaggio & Powell (1983 [1991]); Brunsson & Sahlin-Andersson (2000).
88. For example, Brunsson (1997); Røvik (1996).
89. For example, Czarniawska & Joerges (1996); Sahlin-Andersson (1996); Røvik (2000).
90. For example, Abrahamson (1996).
91. Barley & Kunda (1992).
92. Brunsson & Olsen (1998).
93. Brunsson & Sahlin-Andersson (2000).
94. Czarniawska & Joerges (1996).

95. Furusten & Lerdell (1998).
96. Similar problematics are discussed by Tamm Hallström (2004) in a study on standardization organizations' battle to gain authority.
97. KKR (2000a, p. 17).
98. KKR (2000a).
99. KKR (2000b, pp. 15–19).
100. Furusten (2000).
101. Meyer & Rowan (1977 [1991]); Jepperson (1991).
102. Carlson (1951 [1991], p. x).

References

Abrahamson, E. (1996), 'Technical and aesthetic fasion', in B. Czarniawska & G. Sevón (eds), *Translating Organizational Change*, New York: Walter de Gruyter, pp. 117–138.

Ahrne, G. & Brunsson, N. (eds) (2004), *Regelexplosionen*, Stockholm: EFI.

Almqvist, R. (2006), *New Public Management*, Lund: Liber.

Barley, S. & Kunda, G. (1992), 'Design and devotion: surges of rational and normative ideologies of control in managerial discourse', *Administrative Science Quarterly*, 37, 363–399.

Brint, S. (1994), *In an Age of Experts: The Changing Role of Professionals in Politics and Public Life*, Princeton: Princeton University Press.

Brunsson, N. (ed.) (1981), 'Fëretagsekonomi – sanning eller moral? Om det normativa i fëretagsekonomisk idéutveckling', Studentlitteratur.

Brunsson, N. (1989), *The Organization of Hypocrisy, Talk Decision and Actions in Organizations*, Chichester: Wiley & Sons.

Brunsson, N. (1991), 'Politisering och företagisering. Institutionell förankring och förvirring i organisationernas värld in Arvidsson-Lind, Ledning av företag och förvaltningar', Stockholm: SNS.

Brunsson, N. (1997), 'The standardization of organizational forms as a cropping-up process', *Scandinavian Journal of Management*, 13 (3), 307–320.

Brunsson, N. & Olsen, J.P. (1998), *The Reforming Organization*, Bergen: Fagbokforlaget.

Brunsson, N. & Sahlin-Andersson, K. (2000), 'Constructing organizations: the example of public sector reform', *Organization Studies*, 21 (4), 721–746.

Burrell, G. & Morgan, G. (1979), *Sociological Paradigms in Organizational Analysis*, London: Heinemann Educational Books.

Carlson, S. (1951 [1991]), *Executive Behaviour. Reprinted with Contributions by Henry Mintzberg and Rosemary Stewart*, Acta Universitatis Upsaliensis. Studia Oeconomiae Negotiorum 32, Stockholm: Almqvist & Wiksell International.

Carlzon, J. (1985), *Riv Pyramiderna*, Stockholm: Bonniers.

Christensen, T. & Lægreid, P. (eds) (2001), *New Public Management. The Transformation of Ideas and Practice*, London: Ashgate.

Clark, R. (1995), *Managing Consultants*, London: Open University Press.

Clark, T. & Fincham, R. (eds) (2001), *Critical Consulting: New Perspectives on the Management Advice Industry*, Oxford: Blackwell.

Coase, R.H. (1937), 'The nature of the firm', *Economica*, 4, 386–405.

Cyert, R. & March, J. (1963), *A Behavioral Theory of the Firm*, Engelwood Cliffs, NJ: Prentice-Hall.

Czarniawska-Joerges, B. (1988), *Att Handla Med Ord*, Stockholm: Carlsson Bokförlag.

Czarniawska-Joerges, B. (1985), 'The ugly sister: on relationship between the private and the public sector in Sweden, *Scandinavian Journal of Management Studies*, 2 (2), 83–103.

Czarniawska, B. & Joerges, B. (1996), 'Travels of ideas', in B. Czarniawska & G. Sevón (eds), *Translating Organizational Change*, New York: Walter de Gruyter, pp. 13–48.

Czarniawska, B. & Sevón, G. (1996), 'Introduction', in B. Czarniawska & G. Sevón (eds), *Translating Organizational Change*, New York: Walter de Gruyter, pp. 1–12.

Czarniawska, B. & Sevón, G. (eds) (2005), *Global Ideas – How Ideas, Objects and Practices Travel in the Global Economy*, Copenhagen: CBS Press.

DiMaggio, P. & Powell, W. (1983 [1991]), 'The iron cage revisited: institutional isomorphism and collective rationality', in W. Powell & P. DiMaggio (eds), *The New Institutionalism in Organizational Analysis*, Chicago: The University of Chicago Press, pp. 147–160. (Originally published in *American Sociological Review*, 48 (2), April 1983, 147–160.)

DiMaggio, P. & Powell, W. (eds) (1991), *The New Institutionalism in Organizational Analysis*, Chicago: The University of Chicago Press.

Djelic, M.-L. (1998), *Exporting the American Model*, Oxford: Oxford University Press.

Djelic, M.-L. & Quack, S. (2003), *Globalization and Institutions: Redefining the Rules of the Economic Game*, Cheltenham, UK, and Northampton, MA, USA: Edward Elgar.

Djelic, M.-L. & Sahlin-Andersson, K. (eds) (2006), *Transnational Governance*, Cambridge, UK: Cambridge University Press.

Engelsson, M. (2006), 'Lost and added in translation – a case study of the strategies used to implement a market reform in a Chinese state administration', Stockholm: Stockholm School of Economics, Department of Management and Organizations, Master Thesis.

Engwall, L., Furusten, S. & Wallerstedt, E. (2002), 'Professors as management consultants', in M. Kipping & L. Engwall (eds), *Management Consulting: Emergence and Dynamics of a Knowledge Industry*, Oxford: Oxford University Press, pp. 36–51.

Fernler, K. (1994), 'Generella modeller och lokala lösningar', in B. Jacobsson (ed.), *Organisationsexperiment i Kommuner och Landsting*, Stockholm: Nerenius & Santérus förlag, pp. 93–117.

Fernler, K. (1996), *Mångfald eller Likriktning*, Stockholm: Nerenius & Santérus förlag.

Fincham, R. (ed.) (1996), *New Relationships in the Organised Professions*, Aldershot: Avebury.

Forssell, A. (1992), *Moderna tider i Sparbanken (Modern Times in the Savings Bank)*, Stockholm: Nerenius & Santérus förlag.

Forssell, A. & Jansson, D. (2000), 'Idéer som fängslar: recept för en offentlig reformation', Lund: Liber Ekonomi.

Forssell, A. & Norén, L. (2006), 'Konkurrens på likvärdiga villkor på offentliga marknader', *Nordiska Organisasjonsstudier*, 1, 7–31.

Foucault, M. (1971 [1993]), 'Diskursens ordning (L'ordre du discours)', Rönneholm: Brutus Östling bokförlag symposium.

Furusten, K. (2009), *Det Förändrade Kontraktet, Banker och Kundkonkurser under 1990-talets Finanskris*, Uppsala: Företagsekonomiska Institutionen (Diss).

Furusten, S. (1996), *Den Populära Managementkulturen*, Stockholm, Nerenius & Santérus förlag.

Furusten, S. (1999), *Popular Management Books – How They are Made and What They Mean for Organisations*, London: Routledge.

Furusten, S. (2000), 'The knowledge base of standards', in N. Brunsson & B. Jacobsson (eds), *A World of Standards*, Oxford: Oxford University Press, pp. 71–84.

Furusten, S. (2002), 'Från idé till institution', in H. Hasselblardh & E. Beijerot (eds), *Kvalitetens Gränser*, Lund: Academia Adacta, pp. 19–39.

Furusten, S. (2003), *God Managementkonsultation – Reglerad Expertis Eller Improviserat Artisteri*, Lund: Studentlitteratur.

Furusten, S. (2005), 'Reglering utan regler – normer för managementkonsultation', in K. Nilsson, K. Fernler & R. Henning (eds), *En Illusion av Frihet*, Lund: Studentlitteratur, pp. 163–184.

Furusten, S. & Lerdell, D. (1998), 'Managementiseringen av förvaltningen', in G. Ahrne (ed.), *Stater som Organisationer*, Stockholm: Nerenius & Santérus förlag, pp. 99–122.

Furusten, S. & Werr, A. (eds) (2005), *Dealing with Confidence – The Construction of Need and Trust* in *Management Advisory Services*, Copenhagen: CBS Press.

Galbraith, J. (1973), *Designing Complex Organizations*, Reading, MA: Addison-Wesley.

Gammelsætter, H. (1994), 'Divisionalization: structure or process. A longitudinal perspective', *Scandinavian Journal of Management*, 10 (3), 331–346.

Giddens, A. (1990), *The Consequences of Modernity*, Stanford: Stanford University Press.

Greenwood, R., Oliver, C., Sahlin, K. & Suddaby, R. (eds) (2008), *The Sage Handbook of Organizational Institutionalism*, London: Sage.

Greiner, L. & Metzger, R. (1983), *Consulting to Management*, Englewood Cliffs, NJ: Prentice-Hall.

Gummesson, E. (1991), *Qualitative Methods in Management Research*, London: Sage.

Hägg, I. & Johanson, J. (eds) (1982), *Företag i Nätverk – Ny Syn På Konkurrenskraft* (Enterprise in Network), Stockholm: SNS.

Hatch, M.-J. (1999), 'Exploring the empty spaces of organizing: how improvisational jazz helps re-describe organizational structure,' *Organization Studies*, 20 (1), 75–100.

Hood, C. (1995), '"The New Public Management" in the 1980s: variations on a theme', *Accounting, Organizations and Society*, 20 (2/3), 93–109.

Jacobsson, B. (1994), *Organisationsexperiment i Kommuner och Landsting*, Stockholm: Nerenius & Santérus förlag.

Jepperson, R. (1991), 'Institutions, institutional effects and institutionalism', in W. Powell & P. DiMaggio (eds), *The New Institutionalism in Organizational*

Analysis, Chicago: The University of Chicago Press, pp. 143–163.

Kieser, A. (2002), 'On communication barriers between management science, consultancies and business companies', in T. Clark & R. Fincham (eds), *Critical Consulting. New Perspectives on the Management Advice Industry*, Oxford: Blackwell, pp. 206–227.

Kipping, M. & Engwall, L. (eds) (2002), *Management Consultation*, Oxford: Oxford University Press.

Kipping, M., Furusten, S. & Gammelsaeter, H. (2003), 'Converging towards American dominance? Developments and structures of the consultancy fields in Western Europe', Reading: University of Reading, Department of Economics, Entreprise et Histoire, No. 33, pp. 25–40.

KKR (National Council for Quality and Development) (2000a), 'Kvalitetsarbete i staten', utredning beställd av Statens Kvalitets – och kompetensutvecklingsråd.

KKR (National Council for Quality and Development) (2000b), 'Kvalitetsutveckling för statlig förvaltning – förutsättningar och behov', utredning beställd av Statens Kvalitets – och kompetensutvecklingsråd.

Kubr, M. (ed.) (1996), *Management Consulting: A Guide to the Profession – Third (revised) Edition*, Geneva: ILO.

Kuhn, T.S. (1962 [1970]), *The Structure of Scientific Revolutions*, Chicago: The University of Chicago Press.

Lane, J.-E. (2000), *New Public Management*, London: Routledge.

Latour, B. (1987), *Science in Action*, Bristol: Open University Press.

Lindberg, K. (2005), 'Beordrad självreglering eller frivilliga direktiv? Hur man tog fram en svensk standard för ägarstyrning', in K. Svedberg-Nilsson, K. Fernler & R. Henning (eds), *En Illusion av Frihet*, Lund: Studentlitteratur, pp. 27–48.

Lindberg, K. & Furusten, S. (2005), 'Breaking laws, making deals', in S. Furusten & A. Werr (eds), *Dealing with Confidence*, Copenhagen: CBS Press, pp. 169–183.

McCloskey, D. (1986), *The Rhetorics of Economics*, Brighton: Harvester Press.

Meyer, A., Frost, P. & Weick, K.E. (1998), 'The Organization Science Jazz Festival: improvisation as a metaphor for organizing: overture', *Organization Science*, 9 (5), 540–542.

Meyer, J. (1994), 'Rationalized environments', in R. Scott & J. Meyer (eds), *Institutional Environments and Organizations*, London: Sage, pp. 28–54.

Meyer, J. (1996), 'Otherhood, the promulgation and transmission of ideas in the modern organizational environment', in B. Czarniawska & G. Sevón (eds), *Translating Organizational Change*, New York: Walter de Gruyter, pp. 241–252.

Meyer, J.W., Nagel, J. & Snyder, Jr., C.W. (1993), 'The expansion of mass education in Botswana: local and world society perspectives', *Comparative Education Review*, 37, 454–475.

Meyer, J.W. & Rowan, B. (1977 [1991]), 'Institutionalized organizations: formal structure as myth and ceremony', in W. Powell & P. DiMaggio (eds), *The*

New Institutionalism in Organizational Analysis, Chicago: The University of Chicago Press, pp. 41–62.

Morgan, G, (1986), *Images of Organization*, London: Sage.

Normann, R. (1975), *Skapande Företagsledning*, Lund: Aldus.

Normann, R. (1982 [2001]), *Service Management*, Lund: Liber.

Pasmore, W. (1998), 'Organizing for jazz', *Organization Science*, 9 (5), 562–568.

Proposition (1997/98:136), *Statlig Förvaltning i Medborgarnas Tjänst*, regeringskansliet.

Rhenman, E. (1973), *Organization Theory for Long-Range Planning*, London: Wiley & Sons.

Ritzer, G. (1993), *The McDonaldization of Society: An Investigation into the Changing Character of Contemporary Social Life*, Thousand Oaks, CA: Pine Forge Press.

Rombach, B. (1999), *Den Marknadslika Kommunen*, Stockholm: Nerenius & Santérus förlag.

Røvik, K.A. (1996), 'Deinstitutionalization and the logic of fashion', in B. Czarniawska & G. Sevón (eds), *Translating Organizational Change*, New York: Walter de Gruyter, pp. 139–172.

Røvik, K.A. (2000), *Moderna Organisationer*, Lund: Liber.

Sahlin-Andersson, K. (1996), 'Imitating by editing success: the construction of organizational fields', in B. Czarniawska & G. Sevón (eds), *Translating Organizational Change*, New York: Walter de Gruyter, pp. 69–92.

Sahlin-Andersson, K. & Engwall, L. (eds) (2002), *The Expansion of Management Knowledge: Carriers, Flows and Sources*, Stanford: Stanford University Press.

Sahlin-Andersson, K. & Sevón, G. (2003), 'Imitation and identification as performatives', in B. Czarniawska & G. Sevón (eds), *The Northern Lights: Organization Theory in Scandinavia*, Lund: Liber, pp. 249–266.

Saint-Martin, D. (2000), *Building the new managerialist state*, Oxford: Oxford University Press.

Scott, R.W. (1995), *Institutions and Organizations*, London: Sage.

Sevón, G. (1996), 'Organizational imitation in identity transformation', in B. Czarniawska & G. Sevón (eds), *Translating Organizational Change*, New York: Walter de Gruyter, pp. 49–68.

Sjögren, E. (2006), *Reasonable Drugs*, Stockholm: EFI.

Smith, A. (1776 [2001]), *An Inquiry into the Nature and Causes of the Wealth of Nations*, London: www.adamsmith.org/smith/won.

SOU (1997:57), *I Medborgarnas Tjänst*, Förvaltningspolitiska kommissionens slutbetänkande.

Strang, D. & Meyer, J. (1994), 'Institutional conditions for diffusion', in R. Scott & J. Meyer (eds), *Institutional Environments and Organizations*, London: Sage, pp. 100–112.

Sturdy, A. (1997), 'The consultancy process – an insecure business', *Journal of Management Studies*, 34 (3), 389–413.

Svedberg-Nilsson, K., Fernler, K. & Henning, R. (eds) (2005), *En Illusion av Frihet*, Lund: Studentlitteratur.

Tamm Hallström, K. (2004), *Organizing International Standarization*, Cheltenham, UK and Northampton, MA, USA: Edward Elgar.

Von Wright, G. (1993), *Myten om Framsteget*, Stockholm: Bonniers.

Whitley, R. (1984), *The Intellectual and Social Organization of the Sciences*, Oxford: Oxford University Press.

Williamsson, O.E. (1975), *Markets and Hierarchies. Analysis and Antitrust Implications*, New York: The Free Press.

Internet

www.skb.se, 2007-02-13.
www.ivf.se, 2007-05-16.
www.vv.se, 2007-05-16.

Index